WORKING LIFE: EMPLOYEE ATTITUDES AND ENGAGEMENT 2006

Catherine Truss

Emma Soane

Christine Edwards

Karen Wisdom

Andrew Croll

Jamie Burnett

The Chartered Institute of Personnel and Development is the leading publisher of books and reports for personnel and training professionals, students, and all those concerned with the effective management and development of people at work.
For full details of all our titles, please contact the Publishing Department:
Tel: 020 8612 6204
E-mail: publish@cipd.co.uk

To view and purchase all CIPD titles:
www.cipd.co.uk/bookstore

For details of CIPD research projects:
www.cipd.co.uk/research

WORKING LIFE: EMPLOYEE ATTITUDES AND ENGAGEMENT 2006

Catherine Truss

Emma Soane

Christine Edwards

KINGSTON BUSINESS SCHOOL, KINGSTON UNIVERSITY

Karen Wisdom

Andrew Croll

Jamie Burnett

IPSOS MORI

First published 2006
Reprinted 2007

Cover and text design by Sutchinda Rangsi-Thompson
Typeset by Paperweight
Printed in Great Britain by Antony Rowe

British Library Cataloguing in Publication Data
A catalogue record for this book is available from the British Library

ISBN   1 84398 179 3
ISBN-13   978 1 84398 179 4

Chartered Institute of Personnel and Development,
151 The Broadway, London SW19 1JQ

Tel: 020 8612 6200
Website: www.cipd.co.uk

Incorporated by Royal Charter. Registered charity no. 1079797.

CONTENTS

LIST OF CHARTS, FIGURES AND TABLES

FOREWORD

The CIPD has been undertaking national surveys of employee attitudes at roughly annual intervals for more than a decade. They have consistently presented a reliable picture of the changing employment relationship and countered many myths about, for example, employee satisfaction, job security and careers.

But this report breaks new ground in a number of ways. First, it focuses on the headline findings about what is happening in today's labour market and presents the numbers in an easily accessible graphical format. Second, it uses a robust model of employee engagement to interpret what is happening. Third, it provides managers with detailed advice on the practical implications of the findings.

Employee engagement has become the new management mantra: everybody wants it. But what is it, and how can you get it? This report makes an important contribution to demystifying the subject for HR students and practitioners.

Put simply, engagement means feeling positive about your job. This translates into positive outcomes both for employer and employees. The report breaks engagement down into three components:

❖ emotional – being very involved with one's work

❖ cognitive – focusing very hard while at work

❖ physical – being willing to 'go the extra mile'.

Employers need engaged employees because they can act as organisational advocates and help promote their organisation as an 'employer of choice'.

But the key for managers is knowing how to set about leveraging an engaged workforce. Based on the survey findings, the report concludes that the three main drivers of employee engagement are:

❖ having opportunities to feed your views upwards

❖ feeling well informed about what is happening in the organisation

❖ thinking that your manager is committed to your organisation.

The ability to give upward feedback is sometimes called employee 'voice'. But this should not be confused with the existence of machinery for consulting or communicating with employees. The basic issue is how far management is listening to what employees say, and what if anything they are doing about it.

Managerial fairness in dealing with problems and treating employees with respect don't appear to feed directly into engagement but do affect performance and employees' intention to stay.

There is no 'off-the-peg' solution to increasing employee engagement. The report emphasises that different groups of employees are influenced by different factors, and managers need to find out what matters to their own staff. The CIPD is happy to make available the questions used in the survey on which this report is based, and the 'top-line' percentage responses, so that organisations can use them to benchmark their own survey results (please email: research@cipd.co.uk).

Another 'first' in this year's survey is an examination of the experience of different groups of employees. The good news is that women tend to be more engaged than men and older workers more engaged than younger workers. Managers too are more engaged than other workers. And workers on flexible contracts are more emotionally engaged, more satisfied with their work and more likely to speak positively about their organisation.

However, two groups have a more negative experience of work. Employees with a disability are less happy with their work–life balance than other workers; experience more bullying and harassment; are more likely to say they are not listened to; and feel more stressed and pressured. And public sector workers report more bullying and harassment than those in the private sector; are less satisfied with the opportunities they have to use their abilities; feel more stressed and pressured; and are more critical of their organisation.

So looking at the findings as a whole, how are managers doing at the job of managing their people? Basically, not too well. The report finds that levels of engagement are higher than some other studies have suggested: in this survey, over one-third of employees are actively engaged with their work. But a significant minority of people have a very low opinion of their senior managers and perceive them as untrustworthy. A large number also see senior managers as lacking in vision. Nearly half of all employees are either looking around for another job or are in the process of leaving.

The conclusion has to be that many organisations have problems with visibility, communication and involvement. Senior managers can make a real difference to working lives and organisational performance by strengthening employee involvement.

The messages in this report deserve the widest possible readership. A summary version of the report entitled 'How engaged are British employees?' can be downloaded from the CIPD website (see www.cipd.co.uk/surveys). A series of essays on the findings by specialists in key areas addressed by the survey is being published as 'Reflections on employee engagement' (see www.cipd.co.uk/changeagendas).

This report is the work of Kingston Business School and Ipsos MORI. The CIPD is extremely grateful to both organisations for the professional care and application they have shown in producing a thorough and accessible report against demanding timescales. Thanks are due in particular to Professor Katie Truss of Kingston Business School and Karen Wisdom of Ipsos MORI for their management of the research. With the help of the CIPD's own Publishing Department, the research team has succeeded in translating statistical analysis into a highly readable and visually attractive product.

Mike Emmott
CIPD Adviser, Employee Relations

EXECUTIVE SUMMARY

This report is based on the findings of a nationwide survey of employee attitudes and engagement that was conducted electronically during July 2006, using a stratified sample of 2,000 employees from across the UK. The report is the latest in a long-running series by the CIPD and provides an independent picture of the experience of work in the UK.

Employee engagement, or 'passion for work', involves feeling positive about your job as well as being prepared to go the extra mile to make sure you do your job to the best of your ability. Perhaps not surprisingly, high levels of engagement have been found to be associated with a whole range of beneficial outcomes, including high levels of performance. It has come to be seen as one of the most important ways of measuring how employees feel about their work today.

Engagement has three dimensions: *emotional* engagement, being very involved emotionally with one's work; *cognitive* engagement, focusing very hard while at work; and *physical* engagement, being willing to 'go the extra mile' for your employer.

We wanted to find out how employees in the UK feel about their work and, crucially, what employers can do to raise levels of engagement. We found that:

❖ 35% of employees are engaged with their work

❖ levels of engagement among the under-35s are significantly lower than those in the older age groups

❖ engaged employees perform better than others, are more likely to recommend their organisation to others, take less sick leave and are less likely to quit

❖ engaged employees also experience increased job satisfaction and more positive attitudes and emotions generally towards their work, suggesting that enhanced levels of engagement are of benefit to the individual as well as their employer.

The main drivers of employee engagement are:

❖ having opportunities to feed your views upwards

❖ feeling well-informed about what is happening in the organisation

❖ thinking that your manager is committed to your organisation.

We also found that:

❖ women are more engaged with their work than men

❖ older employees are more engaged than younger employees.

Perceived managerial fairness in dealing with problems also significantly affects individual performance, although it is not significantly related to engagement.

In our survey we collected information about a whole range of issues in order to build up a complete picture of attitudes to working life in the UK. Our findings are grouped into sections on working life: management, leadership and communication; attitudes to work; engagement; and outcomes in terms of performance, intention to quit and sickness absence. The main findings are summarised below.

WORKING LIFE

❖ One in ten employees works 50+ hours a week.

❖ While 24% of people are unhappy with their work–life balance, 29% feel their organisations help them achieve the correct work–life balance.

❖ Employees who are satisfied with their work–life balance and those on flexible contracts are more engaged with their work than those who are dissatisfied or not working flexibly.

❖ Women, over-55s, part-timers and those working in small organisations are happier with their work–life balance than others.

❖ People who take less annual leave than they are entitled to are more engaged in their work but do not achieve higher levels of performance.

❖ Nineteen per cent of employees overall and 29% of black and Asian employees have experienced some form of bullying or harassment in the last two years.

❖ Those who have experienced bullying or harassment are, understandably, more likely to be depressed and anxious, to be less satisfied with their work, to have a low opinion of their managers and senior managers, and to want to leave their organisation.

MANAGEMENT, LEADERSHIP AND COMMUNICATION

❖ People are generally unhappy with the way they are managed and with the senior leadership of their organisation.

❖ Thirty-two per cent say that their manager rarely or never discusses their training and development needs with them, 30% rarely or never get feedback on their performance and 25% are rarely or never made to feel their work counts.

❖ Some 41% of employees get feedback on how they are performing; those who get more feedback tend to perform better.

❖ Fifty per cent of employees are confident that, if they have a problem at work, it will be dealt with fairly.

❖ Forty-eight per cent feel that their senior managers have a clear vision of where the organisation is going, 37% have confidence in their senior management team and 34% trust their senior managers.

❖ Thirty-eight per cent of employees say that directors and senior managers treat employees with respect.

❖ Forty-two per cent of people do not feel they are kept well informed about what is going on in their organisation.

❖ Thirty-seven per cent of people are satisfied with the opportunities they have to feed their views and opinions upwards.

❖ Those with positive views about their managers and senior managers are most engaged with their work, perform better and are less likely to quit.

ATTITUDES TO WORK

❖ Just over half of people, 52%, say that their work is personally meaningful to them and that they are satisfied with their job.

❖ People derive a great deal of their job satisfaction from their co-workers, to whom 89% feel very loyal.

❖ Only 40% of employees are satisfied with relations between managers and employees in their organisation, while 27% are satisfied with the way their organisation is managed. Just under a quarter, 23%, are satisfied with their opportunities for promotion.

❖ Some 45% are satisfied with their opportunities to use their abilities.

❖ About a fifth of employees, 22%, experience high levels of stress, and nearly half, 44%, say that they feel under excessive pressure once or twice a week or more.

❖ Only 6% of employees look forward all of the time to going to work, and 26% rarely or never look forward to going to work.

❖ However, people feel very loyal towards their organisation, 74% saying that they feel some or a great deal of loyalty, and 65% saying that they feel committed to helping their organisation achieve its objectives.

ENGAGEMENT

❖ More women than men are engaged with their work: 37%, compared with 34%.

❖ Only 26% of under-35s report feeling engaged, compared with 41% of over-35s.

❖ Whereas 46% of managers are engaged, only 29% of non-managers are.

❖ Of the three types of engagement, levels of emotional engagement are the highest, 58% of employees being emotionally engaged (feeling engrossed in their work), while 31% are cognitively engaged (focusing very hard on their work) and 38% are physically engaged (willing to go the extra mile).

❖ Engaged employees are more likely to act as organisational advocates than disengaged employees and therefore may have a powerful role to play in promoting their organisation as an employer of choice.

OUTCOMES

❖ Most people, 74%, reported that their most recent appraisal rating was 'good' or 'excellent'.

❖ Almost half of employees, 47%, are looking for another job or are in the process of leaving; just under one quarter of employees expect to leave within the year.

❖ The most common reason for quitting is insufficient pay, followed by low job satisfaction.

❖ While 82% of employees say they take 5 days or fewer sick leave per annum, 49% take just one day or none at all.

❖ Workers aged 55+ are significantly less likely to take sick leave than younger workers.

❖ Rates of sickness absence are higher in the public sector than the private, and public sector workers also experience more bullying and harassment and report higher levels of stress and pressure than their private sector counterparts.

❖ Engaged employees take less sick leave than disengaged employees.

❖ Engaged employees are less likely to leave their employer than disengaged employees.

DEMOGRAPHIC DIFFERENCES

❖ Although differences have emerged between groups of employees, demographic variables alone are not predictors of levels of engagement or performance. A positive working environment and sound management practice are the key to fostering high levels of engagement and performance for everyone.

Gender

❖ Women are more engaged with their work than men and are more satisfied; they feel more positively about their senior management team and are more loyal.

❖ Women are more likely to act as organisational advocates than men.

❖ Women work shorter hours, are happier with their work–life balance and feel they get more support in this than do men.

❖ Women experience more bullying and harassment than men.

❖ Women report higher performance appraisal ratings than men.

Age

❖ Workers aged 55+ are more engaged than younger employees and also take less sick leave.

❖ Employees aged under 35 are the least engaged.

❖ Workers under 25 have more trust and confidence in their senior management team than older workers.

Disability

❖ Employees with a disability tend to work a shorter week but are less happy with their work–life balance.

❖ They experience more bullying and harassment than others and feel less supported if they have a problem.

❖ They are also more likely to say that they are not listened to, are less satisfied with their work, and are more stressed and pressured than others. They feel less control over their work

and report being more anxious. They are also more critical of their organisation than others.

❖ They are less likely to have been rated good or excellent in their performance appraisal, and are less likely than employees without a disability to remain in their job.

❖ Employees with a disability rate their own performance lower than those without a disability and also report higher instances of long periods of sick leave.

Managers

❖ Managers work longer hours and tend to take less holiday than other workers. They also feel less happy about their work–life balance but earn more than non-managers.

❖ Managers feel more positive about communication and involvement, and feel they have more support and recognition and are listened to more than non-managers.

❖ More managers have had an appraisal during the past year than other employees and are more likely to report they are treated fairly at work.

❖ However, they are less likely to believe senior managers have a vision.

❖ Managers find their work more important and more meaningful than non-managers do.

❖ Overall, they are more satisfied with their work but also report they are more stressed and anxious. They report more loyalty to their organisation than non-managers and are more likely to look forward to coming to work.

❖ Managers are also significantly more engaged with their work than non-managers.

❖ Managers report higher performance appraisal ratings than non-managers and rate their own performance more highly. They say they are less likely to leave their organisation than non-managers and also are more hopeful of promotion.

Workers on flexible contracts

❖ Those on flexible contracts tend to be more emotionally engaged, more satisfied with their work, more likely to speak positively about their organisation and less likely to quit than those not employed on flexible contracts. However, there are no differences in terms of reported performance.

❖ Flexible workers tend to feel that they get help from their employer in managing their work–life balance. However, they also have much more positive views about their immediate manager than those not on flexible contracts and are more loyal to their organisation, as well as more likely to act as organisational advocates.

❖ Employees on flexible contracts are more likely to report that their work is important and meaningful to them than those not on flexible contracts. They feel they are treated more fairly and listened to more than other workers do, and they are also more likely to take part in discussions about their training and development needs.

❖ Flexible workers are more likely to stay with their employer and to rate their chances of promotion highly.

Sector

❖ We found no differences between the public and the private sectors in terms of hours worked; however, public sector workers are more likely to receive some compensation for working extra hours than those in the private sector.

❖ We would have expected that public sector workers would receive more help from their employer to achieve a good work–life balance, but actually there is no difference.

❖ Public sector workers report more bullying and harassment than those in the private sector, are less satisfied with the opportunities they have to use their abilities, feel more stressed and pressured, and are more critical of their organisation than those in the private sector.

❖ Public sector employees are more likely not to feel that their senior managers have a clear vision for the organisation and have less trust and confidence in their senior managers. They are also less likely to believe organisational communication.

❖ More public sector workers find their work worthwhile and personally meaningful than do private sector employees.

❖ Public sector workers rate their own performance lower than private sector employees do, and take more sick leave.

MANAGEMENT IMPLICATIONS

Given the clear association between engagement, job satisfaction, advocacy and performance, there is every incentive for managers to seek to drive up levels of engagement among the workforce. We recommend employers consider the following:

❖ Allowing people the opportunity to feed their views and opinions upwards is the single most important driver of engagement.

❖ Keeping employees informed about what is going on in the organisation is critical.

❖ Employees need to see that managers are committed to the organisation in order to feel engaged themselves.

❖ Having fair and just management processes for dealing with problems is important in driving up levels of performance.

❖ Different groups of employees are influenced by different combinations of factors, and managers need to consider carefully what is most important to their own staff, beyond the more general messages contained in this report.

In addition to the general issues around engagement, many other points have emerged through the study that are significant for managers. There is much that employers can do to enhance the working experiences of their staff, as well as to improve levels of engagement and performance.

Working life

Working conditions have important effects on levels of engagement, performance and intentions to quit. There is much that managers can do to create a more positive environment where employees can flourish.

❖ Create opportunities for people to work flexibly, as this will raise levels of engagement, satisfaction and advocacy, and improve retention rates; those with a good work–life balance are more engaged.

❖ Allow employees a degree of choice in terms of how they manage their work–life balance, as this is important to individual well-being.

❖ Work–life balance is important for *all* employees, including those who are often neglected in discussions over this issue, such as men, managers and those with a disability. Long working hours are detrimental to health and do not lead to higher levels of performance.

❖ Dissatisfaction with pay will often lead people to quit; a sound pay policy, including benchmarking surveys, is therefore critical to retain top performers.

❖ More important than pay, however, is whether or not the content of the job is meaningful to the individual; this is true of all forms of work. Managers need to give careful thought as to how jobs are structured, job content and the working environment in order to create meaningful work for everyone, leading to higher levels of engagement and performance.

❖ Bullying and harassment are worryingly prevalent in the workplace, causing poor performance, negative psychological states and high intention to quit; there is therefore an urgent need to address the human and systemic failures that may foster a climate where bullying is acceptable.

Management, leadership and communication

❖ The lack of attention paid by managers to employees' training and development needs is likely to be detrimental to longer-term organisational and individual performance.

❖ Employees need feedback on their performance on a regular basis if they are to understand what is expected of them and how to improve.

❖ People need to feel their work counts in order to perform well.

❖ The ability to consult and involve are critical managerial skills that require more development for a substantial proportion of managers; 18% of employees were found to be 'Uninformed Non-Communicators', receiving little or no information about what is happening in their organisation, and lacking the opportunity for feeding their views upwards.

❖ The management of non-managers appears to be weaker than the management of managers, suggesting that management skills among first-line supervisors are in particular need of being strengthened.

❖ Those on flexible contracts feel much more positive about their line managers than do non-flexible workers, most probably because managers who take the trouble to find ways of helping their staff manage their work–life balance are also those who have better general management skills.

❖ A significant minority of people have a very low opinion of their senior managers and perceive them as untrustworthy; this is likely to be related to matters of visibility, communication and involvement in the workplace. There is an opportunity here for senior management teams to make a real difference to people's working lives and to organisational performance by strengthening employee involvement practices.

❖ A large number also see senior managers as lacking in vision; only 38% can be described as 'Committed Visionaries', both believing that senior managers have a clear vision and being committed themselves to help achieve these objectives.

❖ This suggests that there may be problems of strategy in many organisations and in the communication of strategic vision. It may be more difficult for employees to feel engaged with their work when they do not have a clear understanding of what it is their organisation is trying to achieve.

❖ As nearly half of employees feel they are not well informed about what is going on, organisations need to review their internal communications strategies.

❖ The relatively high level of distrust in the public sector is worrying and may well reflect the amount of change that has affected huge swathes of public sector employees in the UK; senior managers in this sector need to give especial consideration to rectifying this situation.

Attitudes to work

❖ People take their work very seriously; for the majority of people, their work is very important to them. Just over half of people are doing jobs that are personally meaningful, and they are more engaged than others. Managers need to think carefully about the person–job fit when selecting staff, and develop creative ways to make work meaningful.

❖ People who feel positively about their work also tend to feel positively about their organisation and are more engaged. This creates a virtuous circle that managers can foster.

❖ Some 17% of employees are 'Enchanted-Uninvolved': satisfied with their current job but looking for greater

involvement in their organisation. They represent a significant untapped resource.

❖ Almost a third of employees are dissatisfied with employee relations in their organisation; this is an area where managers can usefully deploy their skills to bring about improvements.

❖ Twenty-nine per cent of people are dissatisfied with the opportunities they have to use their abilities, suggesting that managers are missing out on the chance to enhance organisational performance and create jobs that people enjoy.

❖ Nearly a quarter of people feel that their job is very stressful, and nearly half say that they feel under excessive pressure on a frequent basis, which is detrimental to individual and organisational health. Personal appraisals offer managers the opportunity not just to tell employees how they are performing but also to find out how they feel about levels of stress in their job.

❖ Just over a quarter (26%) of people rarely or never look forward to coming to work. As we spend so much of our lives in the workplace, this finding is quite disturbing. Work can be fun, challenging, stimulating, exciting and rewarding for people in all kinds of occupations, leading to employees actually enjoying being at work, rather than regarding it as a painful necessity.

❖ The high degree of loyalty that people feel not just towards their fellow workers but also towards their employers is a cause for optimism. This represents a solid foundation on which to build.

Engagement

❖ We found that levels of engagement are higher than some that other studies have suggested. In this survey 35% of employees are actively engaged with their work. Positive associations between engagement, advocacy, performance and intention to quit mean that it is in employers' interests to drive up levels of engagement among their workforce.

❖ Levels of engagement appear to have significant benefits for employees as well, since engagement is positively associated with job satisfaction and experiences of employment. It is therefore in the interests of employees to work for organisations that positively seek to raise levels of engagement.

❖ Organisations that foster high levels of engagement are more likely to retain high-performing employees.

❖ The fact that younger employees are more disengaged than their older colleagues suggests that organisations are failing to meet the needs of younger workers. This finding has potentially serious long-term consequences for organisations and for the career development of young people, and is an area that merits further research.

❖ While 10% of employees can be described as 'Weak Links', likely to be both critical of their organisation as an employer and unlikely to recommend its products and services, only 37% are 'Champions', scoring positively along both dimensions. This suggests that there is scope for considerable improvement in levels of advocacy in organisations.

Outcomes

❖ The fact that most people feel they have the skills and knowledge needed to do their jobs is encouraging and suggests that employers are giving employees the capabilities they need. However, the fact that many do not feel satisfied with the opportunities they are given to use their abilities suggests that some are over-qualified for the jobs they are doing currently, or that they are not reaching their full potential.

❖ The vast majority of employees appear to be performing well, which is also very encouraging; however, only just under a quarter are satisfied with their chances for promotion, which

suggests that today's good performers could become tomorrow's disengaged workers.

❖ Nearly half of all employees are either looking round for another job or are in the process of leaving; this is an extremely high number and suggests that engaged, as well as disengaged, employees are looking for another job. Pay and job satisfaction are the main reasons. Employers need to look proactively at ways of increasing retention rates.

❖ The fact that workers aged 55+ take less sick leave than younger workers runs counter to he popular image of older workers as less reliable. Older workers are also more engaged than younger workers. Given demographic trends and the increasing average age of the workforce, these findings provide encouragement for employers to ensure they foster the enthusiasm, capabilities and dedication of older members of staff.

THE QUEST FOR THE ENGAGED EMPLOYEE

❖ **Our sample of respondents was chosen randomly from an electronic database in order to ensure no bias**

❖ **In reporting differences between groups of employees, we focus only on those differences found to be statistically significant**

❖ **The more positively people feel about their manager and about communication in their organisation, the more engaged they are**

❖ **Managers and leaders can do much to raise levels of engagement within their organisations**

The engaged employee is the passionate employee, the employee who is totally immersed in his or her work, energetic, committed and completely dedicated. You know them when you see them, whether they are working on the checkout at the supermarket, selling houses, leading a team of nurses or heading a multi-million pound enterprise. They are the ones who create a buzz around them, energising their colleagues and clients and generating an aura of success. They are the ones whom employers want to have working for them, rather than for their competitors.

Who are these people, and how do we find them? Are some types of employee more likely to be engaged than others? Can organisations influence levels of engagement among their workforce and, if so, how? These are some of the questions that we set out to answer in this nationwide study of employee engagement.

> '...engagement is likely to be linked to a number of factors that are to do with the people themselves...'

What we know so far is that engagement is likely to be linked to a number of factors that are to do with the people themselves, such as their age or occupation, their experiences of working life, the way they are treated at work, and some of their other attitudes to work, such as job satisfaction. It has also been suggested that levels of engagement affect whether or not someone is likely to quit.

We expected to find that the more positively people feel about their manager and about communication in their organisation, the more engaged they will be, the better they will perform, and the less likely they will be to quit their organisation.

Our survey has borne this out. However, we also found some other, more unexpected, differences between employees, and we reveal what these are during the course of this report. The findings very much reflect the complexity of organisational life and of people's relationship with their work. There are no simple answers!

Before we describe what we found, and offer some suggestions as to why this might be the case, we need to explain in more detail the key areas we have examined. Figure 1 (on page 2) is the model we developed to underpin our research study and to map the relationships we wanted to explore in more detail.

BOX 1: INDIVIDUAL FACTORS

In this part of the model, we looked at a range of demographic variables, such as gender, age, level of education, whether people have dependants, their marital status, ethnic group, and whether or not they have a disability. These individual factors provide us with the information we need to look at how different groups of people feel about their work. Although we stratified the sample to reflect the profile of the national workforce, the number of responses from those from the different ethnic minority groups was correspondingly small. We therefore do not feel confident that testing the significance of differences between the groups is informative, except where we consider issues of bullying and harassment.

BOX 2: WORKING LIFE

This box contains basic information about people's working lives, including their occupation, where they work, their hours of work, annual leave, flexible working arrangements and pay. It also contains vital questions on people's perceptions of their work–life balance, and whether or not they have experienced bullying or harassment at work.

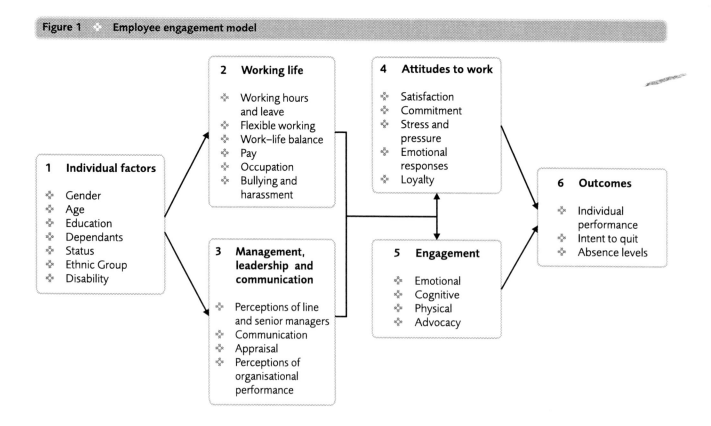

Figure 1 ❖ **Employee engagement model**

1 Individual factors

❖ Gender
❖ Age
❖ Education
❖ Dependants
❖ Status
❖ Ethnic Group
❖ Disability

2 Working life

❖ Working hours and leave
❖ Flexible working
❖ Work–life balance
❖ Pay
❖ Occupation
❖ Bullying and harassment

3 Management, leadership and communication

❖ Perceptions of line and senior managers
❖ Communication
❖ Appraisal
❖ Perceptions of organisational performance

4 Attitudes to work

❖ Satisfaction
❖ Commitment
❖ Stress and pressure
❖ Emotional responses
❖ Loyalty

5 Engagement

❖ Emotional
❖ Cognitive
❖ Physical
❖ Advocacy

6 Outcomes

❖ Individual performance
❖ Intent to quit
❖ Absence levels

BOX 3: MANAGEMENT, LEADERSHIP AND COMMUNICATION

Here, we were concerned with finding out what people think about their managers and leaders, as well as their views on communication within their organisation, opportunity to participate in organisational decision-making and levels of trust. Other research studies have found these factors to be very important in determining levels of engagement, and we wanted to know whether this is also true of our national sample. This is the area where managers are able to have an important influence, and we wanted to find out what the most critical actions are that managers can take to drive higher levels of engagement.

BOX 4: ATTITUDES TO WORK

Some of the most critical aspects of how people feel about their work, and their perceptions of their job, are measured here. We looked at well-being; enthusiasm for work; intrinsic job satisfaction (that is, satisfaction relating to the nature of the work); extrinsic job satisfaction (that is, satisfaction relating to the working conditions); organisational commitment; and experiences of stress and pressure at work.

BOX 5: ENGAGEMENT

Employee engagement is a psychological state that can be described simply as 'passion for work'. However, engagement is a multi-faceted construct, and in order to understand and measure levels of engagement, it can be broken down into three dimensions:[1]

❖ emotional engagement – being involved emotionally with your work

❖ cognitive engagement – focusing very hard on work, thinking about very little else during the working day

❖ physical engagement – being willing to go the extra mile for your employer and put in work over and above contract.[2]

> '...engagement has been found to be good not only for organisations but also for the individuals experiencing it...'

Some people who are very engaged may take this a stage further and speak out as advocates of their organisation and its products or services. And engagement has been found to be good not only for organisations but also for the individuals experiencing it as well, and so having an engaged workforce should be a win–win situation.[3]

BOX 6: OUTCOMES

Finally, we wanted to see how all the factors in our model affect a range of outcomes, including individual performance, intention to leave and sickness absence. Although ideally individual performance would be measured by asking someone else, such as a line manager, about an individual's performance, this is not possible in a survey of this nature, so we asked people how they feel they are performing compared with others, and what rating they received in their most recent performance appraisal.

To sum up, earlier research has suggested that engaged employees are the most productive and the least likely to quit; we wanted to test this out in our survey.

What we are most interested in finding out is what managers can do to drive up levels of engagement in their organisation. The main focus is therefore on the link between box 3 (management, leadership and communication) and box 5 (engagement). We also look at the link between engagement in box 5 and outcomes in box 6, to see whether engaged employees perform better than others, and the link between engagement in box 5 and other employee attitudes in box 4. Finally, we examine the link between box 3 (management, leadership and communication), box 4 (employee attitudes), box 5 (engagement) and the outcomes in box 6.

There is a great deal that managers and leaders can do to raise levels of engagement within their organisations. As subsequent chapters will show, levels of trust and confidence in line and senior managers are disappointingly low in a substantial minority of workplaces. The findings of this survey offer a real opportunity for managers to stand back and evaluate how their own organisation compares with a national sample, and to consider how best they can harness the creative energies of a highly engaged workforce.

Our sample of respondents was chosen randomly from an electronic database to ensure no bias; however, we stratified the sample to ensure it was representative of the British workforce as a whole across such dimensions as age, gender, ethnicity and occupational group. In reporting differences between groups of employees, we focus only on those differences that are found to be statistically significant. More information about the sample and how we collected and analysed the data is presented in the technical appendix (see page 49).

ENDNOTES

1 LUTHANS, F. and PETERSON, S. (2002) Employee engagement and manager self-efficacy. *Journal of Management Development.* Vol 21, No 5/6. pp376–387.

KAHN, W. (1990) Psychological conditions of personal engagement and disengagement at work. *Academy of Management Journal.* Vol 33. pp692–724.

2 MAY, D.R., GILSON, R.L. and HARTER, L.M. (2004). The psychological conditions of meaningfulness, safety and availability and the engagement of the human spirit at work. *Journal of Occupational and Organizational Psychology.* Vol 77. pp11–37.

3 JONES, J. and HARTER, J. (2005) Race effects on the employee engagement-turnover intention relationship. *Journal of Leadership and Organizational Studies.* Vol 11, No 2. pp78–88.

WORKING LIFE

2

❖ **Those in lower-skilled jobs are less engaged than professional groups and managers**

❖ **Those employed flexibly are more engaged but not more likely to report higher performance ratings than others**

❖ **Those working in a mix of locations are more engaged than others**

❖ **Engaged people willingly forgo annual leave and want to remain with their organisation but do not perform more highly than those with a better work–life balance**

❖ **People who feel that they have the correct work–life balance are more engaged with their work**

Conditions of work in terms of pay, hours of work, holidays, flexibility and work–life balance have an enormous impact on how we feel about our work. We hear a great deal in the media about the 'long-hours' culture, and about rising levels of bullying and harassment in the workplace. Is there any evidence that these claims are true? What impact do they have on employees and on levels of engagement and performance?

We start by developing the building-blocks for our model of employee engagement, and we ask: how do working conditions affect levels of engagement, intention to leave and performance? What are the critical areas where management action is needed? The core topics examined were:

❖ occupation

❖ flexible working

❖ location of work

❖ working hours

❖ leave entitlement

❖ work–life balance

❖ pay

❖ bullying and harassment.

OCCUPATION

Our sample reflects the occupational distribution of the workforce as a whole. We used standard classification criteria to group respondents into categories (see Table 1 on page 6).

As expected, significantly more of those in the professional, managerial, skilled trades and operator categories are men, while more women are in the administrative, personal services and retail services categories.

We wanted to know whether there is a link between occupation and engagement.

Key findings

❖ People working in lower-skilled jobs are less engaged in their work than professional groups and managers; this may reflect their experience of working life, rather than their jobs.

❖ No occupations appear to be characterised by higher turnover rates than others.

FLEXIBLE WORKING

I work a term-time contract, when I'm there I work 35 hours a week but I don't work every week of the year, it comes out at 30.2 hours a week on average. I work a flexible day as well. If I need to go early for my children, then I leave early and I might work longer hours another day.

Linda, 42, IT Developer

My employer's attitude to work–life balance is awful. We open every night until 21:30 and we open every Sunday during the year and, really, the order is, if you don't like it, leave.

Deborah, 45, Deputy Manager, Bookmakers

Table 1 ❖ Occupation	
Professional group	%
Professional (eg health, teacher)	22
Administrative and secretarial	21
Associated professional (eg nurse, police officer)	13
Manager or senior official	11
Retail and customer services	10
Skilled trades (eg plumber, electrician)	4
Personal services (eg travel agent, childminder)	4
Process, plant or machine operator	3
Elementary occupations (eg labourer, cleaner)	3

Freedom to have some choice about how to arrange working hours is an issue of great importance to both employers and employees. With recent developments in employment law and cultural shifts in many organisations, there are greater opportunities than ever for employees to fit their work around family and other commitments.

> '...there are greater opportunities than ever for employees to fit their work around family and other commitments.'

In our survey, just over a third (39%) of respondents have at least some degree of flexibility. From the total sample, this breaks down as shown in Chart 1 below.

The previous CIPD Employee Attitude Survey (in 2004) also found that flexible hours was the most common form of flexibility.

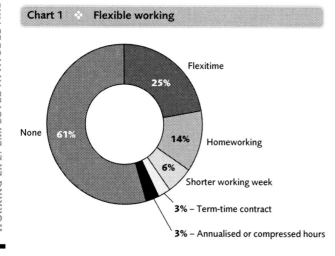

Chart 1   ❖   Flexible working

- Flexitime — 25%
- Homeworking — 14%
- Shorter working week — 6%
- Term-time contract — 3%
- Annualised or compressed hours — 3%
- None — 61%

Term-time contracts are more common in the public sector and among women, while homeworking is significantly more common among managers than non-managers.

A comparison of the groups of people who have flexibility in some form, compared with those who work routine hours and have no flexibility, shows that those employed flexibly are:

❖ more emotionally engaged

❖ more satisfied with their work

❖ more likely to speak positively about their organisation

❖ less likely to quit.

However, they are no more likely to report higher performance ratings than others.

Key finding

❖ Those working on a flexible contract tend to feel much more positively about many aspects of their employment and their employer than those not on a flexible contract, and, in particular, they are more engaged.

LOCATION OF WORK

I found it difficult working from home for the first year, but I find it far easier now than working in the office: there are fewer distractions.

Colin, 45, Account Manager

Another form of flexibility is where you actually do your work. Research has shown that the proportion of employees who work away from the workplace has been rising sharply over recent years, mainly owing to the rapid uptake of increasingly sophisticated IT solutions.[1] Just over half of our sample (55%) said that they spend all their working time in their workplace. However, 45% said that they spend at least some of that time elsewhere. Significantly more women than men spend all their working time at their workplace (59%, compared with 52% of men), which is probably owing to the fact that more men than women work as managers or professionals, which often necessitates travel or working in multiple locations (see Chart 2).

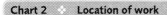

'Significantly more women than men spend all their working time at their workplace...'

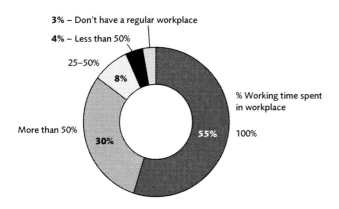

Chart 2 ❖ Location of work

3% – Don't have a regular workplace
4% – Less than 50%
25–50%
8%
More than 50%
30%
55% 100%
% Working time spent in workplace

Does where you work influence how you feel about your work? We looked at the differences between people who work in one location and those who work in a mix of locations, for example spending some time working in an office and some time working at home, or time travelling for work. There are significant differences between these two groups for all forms of engagement; those working in a mix of locations are more engaged than others.

Key findings

❖ There are no differences between people who work in one location and those who work in a mix of locations in terms of their performance appraisal ratings.

❖ There are no differences between people who work in one location compared with those who work in a mix of locations in their intentions to quit or to search for a new job.

WORKING HOURS

I don't take all my leave in order to be seen to be moving things along.

Mike, 47, Manager

Research has often shown that the British work some of the longest hours in Europe, with detrimental effects on both health and lifestyle.[2]

We asked our sample about their working hours and their holidays. Most of our respondents (79%) are contracted to work fewer than 40 hours a week, while 19% are contracted to work 40 to 49 hours, and 2% 50+ hours (see Chart 3).

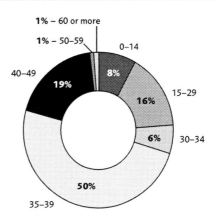

Chart 3 ❖ Weekly contracted hours

1% – 60 or more
1% – 50–59
0–14
40–49
19%
8%
16%
15–29
6%
30–34
50%
35–39

Male employees are significantly more likely (82%) to be contracted to work 35+ hours than women (56%). Some 44% of women are contracted to work fewer than 35 hours a week, compared with just 18% of men.

Part-time work (fewer than 30 hours a week) is more prevalent among public sector than private sector workers. Employees aged 55+ are more likely to be contracted to work 30 hours or fewer than younger workers.

However, we found that many employees are clearly working longer than their contracted hours (see Chart 4 on page 8). While 21% are contracted to work 40+ hours, just over twice as many (43%) report that they are actually working 40+ hours a week. One-third (33%) work 40–49-hour weeks, but just under one-fifth (19%) are actually contracted to do so, and one in ten is working 50+ hours, compared with only 2% contracted to do so. This is particularly worrying, given that research has shown that once you reach the threshold of 40 hours work a week, productivity decreases and people's physical and psychological health may be damaged.[3] Men seem to be working longer hours than women (see Table 2 on page 8).

'Almost twice as many managers as non-managers work 40 hours or more a week...'

There are no significant differences between the public and private sectors in terms of actual hours worked.[4] However, those paid £46,801+ pa are, perhaps not surprisingly, more likely to be working 60+ hours a week than others. Almost twice as many managers as non-managers work 40 hours or more a week: 63% compared with 33%.

Table 2 ❖ Actual weekly hours worked		
%	Men	Women
40+ hours	55	30
50–59 hours	10	4
60+ hours	4	2

Chart 4 ❖ Actual weekly hours worked

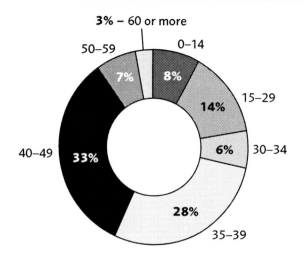

More women than men get time off in lieu, while men are significantly more likely to get neither extra time nor payment for their extra work (42%). This probably reflects the fact that more of the men in our sample (and in the workforce as a whole) are professionals or managers.

It is more common for private sector workers to get no extra rewards for working beyond contract than for their public-sector counterparts (44% compared with 31%). Higher earners, managers and graduates are significantly more likely than other groups to get no extra rewards for extra input.

Key findings

❖ Forty-three per cent of employees work 40+ hours per week, with 10% working 50+ hours.

❖ The longer hours people work, the more stress they report.

LEAVE ENTITLEMENT

Almost all employees (85%) take their full annual leave entitlement (see Chart 6), but women are significantly more likely to do so (88%) than men (83%).

Chart 6 ❖ Full annual leave entitlement taken?

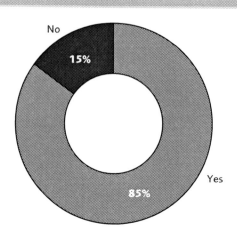

Workers with disabilities are significantly more likely to be working a shorter week of up to 29 hours (39%, compared with 21% of employees without disabilities).

The majority of those who work extra hours are paid extra (32%), get time off in lieu (19%) or both extra time and pay (11%), but a sizeable minority (38%) get neither (see Chart 5).

Chart 5 ❖ Compensation for extra hours worked

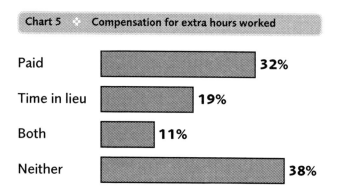

Young and temporary workers tend to be less likely to take all their leave. There are no significant differences between the public and the private sectors here.

Looking at job function, fewer managerial staff than non-managers use up their full holiday allowance: 18% of managers report that they do not take all their leave, compared with 13% of non-managers.

Key finding

❖ Eighteen per cent of managers do not take all their holiday allowance.

Our research suggests that a sizeable minority of employees is working long hours and not taking their full holiday allowance. Those falling into this category also take fewer days off sick (an average of three days in the past year) compared with people who do take their holidays (who took an average of six days off sick in the previous year).

But does this mean that people who put in more time at work do better than their colleagues who take regular annual leave? Are they more engaged in their work, and is this positive for them and their organisations? There are a number of interesting differences between the people who take their annual leave entitlement and those who do not.

Key finding

❖ People who take less annual leave are more engaged in their work and rate themselves as high performers. Yet their actual appraisal ratings are no different from those who do take their leave entitlement.

It seems to make sense that the more engaged someone is in their work, the more motivated they would be to put in long hours. However, in terms of performance rating, these long hours do not make a difference. So, are people who work long hours or who do not take all their annual leave happy to stay with their organisation?

Key finding

❖ People who do not take their holidays are more likely to want to stay with their organisation.

> '...employees who work the longest hours are also the most dissatisfied with their work–life balance and are most at risk of damaging their health and well-being.'

To sum up, engaged people are willing to forgo annual leave in order to continue their work and want to remain with their organisation. However, employees who work the longest hours are also the most dissatisfied with their work–life balance and are most at risk of damaging their health and well-being. They also do not appear to perform any better than those who have achieved a better balance.

WORK–LIFE BALANCE

We do have flexitime. It really does help. It fits in with my lifestyle. My job is always changing and it makes it more interesting. My manager encourages me to do over and above my job, which I enjoy. They are very open and honest. I like that side to it. There are open

communication channels, so that staff can access information. They are very transparent and are always improving the way they operate, and HR are very good at keeping us up to date with salaries and benefits. We have annual conferences where we can interact with the directors and ask them any questions. That's quite a good thing, because you get to meet them and you get to know how they think and how they operate. Morale is high, and people are happy. A lot of people tend to leave and come back to the organisation, so that's always a good sign. I think a lot of people are happy with where they are and their future career. I would definitely recommend it. I wouldn't like to leave the organisation.

Sofya, 24, Marketing Assistant

One area of working life that has received a great deal of attention has been work–life balance.

We asked our respondents whether they feel they achieve the correct balance between their home and work lives. While over half (55%) say yes, nearly a quarter (24%) disagree. This indicates a higher rate of dissatisfaction than was found in the 2004 CIPD Employee Attitudes Survey (see Chart 7).

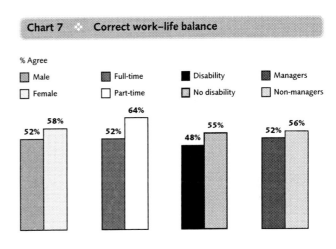

Chart 7 ❖ Correct work–life balance

% Agree

Male | Full-time | Disability | Managers
Female | Part-time | No disability | Non-managers

52% | 58% | 52% | 64% | 48% | 55% | 52% | 56%

It is interesting to note that women are more likely than men to be happy with their work–life balance, which may be due to the fact that more women than men work part-time: 40% compared with 15% (working 34 hours a week or fewer).

It is worrying to see that people with a disability and those with management responsibilities feel they do not have a good work–life balance (see Chart 7 above).

To find out more, we asked our sample whether their organisation provides them with support to help them manage their work–life balance. We found that fewer than one-third (29%) agreed that their organisations do this, while 42% actively disagree (see Chart 8 on page 10). Those who already have flexible arrangements in place and those with children tend to feel more positive.

On the other hand, men, full-timers and managers are more likely to feel they do not get help from their organisation.

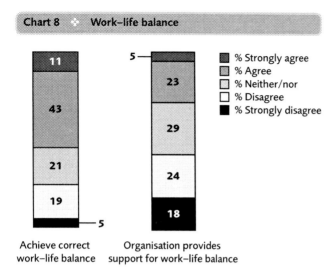

Chart 8   Work–life balance

Legend:
- % Strongly agree
- % Agree
- % Neither/nor
- % Disagree
- % Strongly disagree

Left bar (Achieve correct work–life balance): 11, 43, 21, 19, 5

Right bar (Organisation provides support for work–life balance): 5, 23, 29, 24, 18

Achieve correct work–life balance   Organisation provides support for work–life balance

We note that more men than women say both that they are unhappy with their work–life balance and that they do not get support from their organisation. Given the level of interest in recent years in providing women with more flexible forms of employment, our survey suggests that many organisations have responded positively. Now men seem to be missing out.

> '...more men than women say both that they are unhappy with their work–life balance and that they do not get support from their organisation.'

Interestingly, there are no significant differences between public and private sectors in terms of achieving the correct work–life balance or in receiving employer support, although we might have expected public sector employers to offer more flexibility.

Key findings

❖ Almost a quarter of employees, including many men, those in management roles, full-timers and those with a disability, are not happy with their work–life balance.

❖ Some 42% of people feel that their organisation is not supporting them to improve this.

❖ Men, managers and full-time workers particularly feel they do not get support from their organisation to help them manage their work–life balance.

❖ People who feel that they have the correct work–life balance, and are supported by their organisation to do so, are also more engaged with their work.

PAY

Q: What single change would most improve your working life?

More money: I am poorly paid and living costs are escalating out of control. When will employers wake up and realise this?

More money! In the NHS this year I have had a pay freeze, which means in real terms I am earning far less than I was when I started this job.

Better pay, commensurate with the responsibilities I am constantly asked to assume and the diligence with which I perform my job.

When we asked respondents what the single change was that would most improve their working life, 'More pay!' came the response from most of them. Looking ahead to Chapter 4, we found that just 35% of people are satisfied with what they are paid. As we shall see in Chapter 6, pay is also the most frequently cited reason people want to quit their organisation.

For many employees, receiving more pay is often seen as the solution for numerous unsatisfactory aspects of work. But does paying people more really make that much difference to them, and does it mean that they will be more engaged with their work?

Key finding

❖ Engaged employees are higher-paid employees. Overall, this result probably reflects the fact that those who are paid more are more likely to be in managerial or professional roles, rather than suggesting that pay actually drives engagement. Engaged employees are found in all the occupational groups.

BULLYING AND HARASSMENT

Q: What single change would most improve your working life?

To have a different boss and colleagues. I am constantly bullied at work.

Recognition of bullying in the workplace, with the onus placed on the bully, not the victim.

Reports of bullying and harassment in the workplace are becoming more frequent, and large pay-outs have been made to victims. There have been few systematic surveys of how the experiences of people who have suffered bullying and harassment differ from those who have not. Of particular importance is the difference between ethnic groups and their experiences.

Unfortunately, we found that a high number, nearly one in five employees (19%), have experienced some form of bullying or harassment at work in the last two years. This is most likely to have been bullying, but one in twenty report having experienced violence or the threat of violence at work, and 2% report experiencing sexual harassment or racial harassment (see Chart 9).

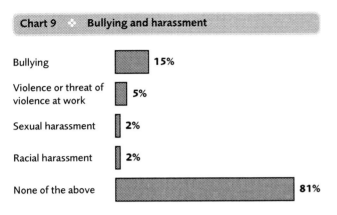

Chart 9 ❖ Bullying and harassment

Bullying — 15%
Violence or threat of violence at work — 5%
Sexual harassment — 2%
Racial harassment — 2%
None of the above — 81%

Women are significantly more likely to have experienced some form of bullying or harassment than men (see Table 3 below).

Workers in the public sector have experienced more bullying or harassment than those in the private sector (22%, compared with 17%), and more have experienced violence or the threat of it (7%, compared with 3%).

Overall, nearly one-third (29%) of Asian employees or those from other ethnic groups report having experienced some form of bullying or harassment, compared with 18% of white employees. Racial harassment is reported by 15% of Asian employees (and 8% among other ethnic groups), but by only 1% of white workers.

Employees with disabilities are at least twice as likely to report having experienced one or more forms of bullying and harassment (37%) compared with non-disabled employees (18%), especially bullying (28%) and violence or the threat of violence (13%). Even racial (9%) and sexual harassment (5%) cases are significantly higher than among those with no disability (only 2%).

We asked in more detail about the type of bullying or harassment that people had experienced. Our sample reports that most of their experiences have been of verbal bullying, with bullying from a manager most common (60% of reported cases), followed by bullying from a colleague (48%). (See Table 4 below.)

Public sector workers who have experienced violence or threats at work are twice as likely as those in the private sector to have experienced them from someone outside the organisation. In contrast, private sector employees are significantly more likely than those in the public sector to have experienced verbal threats from colleagues or from a manager.

Table 3 ❖ Forms of bullying and harassment experienced (last two years)

%	Public	Private	White	Asian/ Asian British	Others	Male	Female	Disability	No disability
Sexual harassment	3	2	2	6	1	1	4	5	2
Racial harassment	2	2	1	15	8	2	2	9	2
Bullying	16	14	14	19	18	11	19	28	14
Violence or threat of violence at work	7	3	5	5	5	5	4	13	4
None of these	78	83	82	71	72	85	76	63	82

Table 4 ❖ Experience of bullying and harassment (last two years)

%	Sexual harassment n=45	Racial harassment n=43	Bullying n=294	Violence/ threat of violence n=97
Verbally, from a manager	49	33	60	16
Verbally, from a colleague	51	56	48	30
Verbally, from someone outside the organisation	24	40	14	57
Physically, from a manager	9	12	4	5
Physically, from a colleague	27	7	4	12
Physically, from someone outside the organisation	9	9	3	39

My boss has a bit of an anger management problem: he tends to shoot the messenger or, if he loses his temper or something annoys him, he will take it out on whoever is in the office. All the managers know about him, but nothing happens. He has a lot on his plate, and most of us just have to tolerate it. On the second day when I was here, I couldn't read his handwriting, and he just exploded in the next room. That kind of thing happens on a daily basis. It is totally unreasonable and contributes to low-level anxiety. I don't like it here. It's quite shocking how it has been ignored.

Jane, 38, Temp

What impact do these worrying levels of bullying have on individuals?

As Jane's story suggests, people who have experienced bullying and harassment:

❖ are much more likely to leave their organisation, and more are actively seeking new jobs

❖ are more depressed and anxious than their counterparts

❖ are less satisfied with their work and find it less meaningful

❖ have a low opinion of their senior managers and communications within their organisation

❖ report having lower appraisal ratings than people not suffering bullying.

Bullying therefore has extremely negative repercussions both for individuals and organisations, and a top priority for all managers has to be the eradication of all forms of bullying and harassment in the workplace.

Key findings

❖ Nineteen per cent of all employees have experienced bullying or harassment.

❖ Some 29% of the non-white respondents report having been bullied or harassed, compared with 18% of white respondents.

❖ More women and those with a disability have experienced bullying or harassment than men and employees without a disability.

ENDNOTES

1 FELSTEAD, A., JEWSON, N. and WALTERS, S. (2005) *Changing places of work*. Basingstoke: Palgrave Macmillan.

2 FOOT, M. and HOOK, C. (2002) *Introducing human resource management*. Harlow: FT Prentice Hall.

3 ARNOLD, J. (2005) *Work psychology*. Harlow: FT Prentice Hall. p398.

4 Throughout the report, 'public sector' also includes employees in the voluntary sector.

MANAGEMENT, LEADERSHIP AND COMMUNICATION

❖ **Supervisors and senior line managers can make or break levels of employee engagement**

❖ **Responses on feedback in this survey were more negative than in the 2004 survey**

❖ **Few respondents agree that senior management have a clear vision of where the organisation is going**

❖ **Public sector workers are more distrustful than their private sector counterparts of senior managers**

Recently we were very busy and a few of us worked a lot of hours to help out, but you didn't get any thanks for it. We're just not appreciated at work. If someone were looking for a job, I wouldn't tell them to get one where I work.

Susan, 43, Customer Service Representative

My manager is very approachable, and if you have an issue, he does try and resolve it as soon as possible.

Sally, 32, Administrator

Management have this attitude of wanting more and more. They just don't care as long as they're making the money.

Lyn, 55, Shop Assistant

One of the most critical factors that influences both how people feel about their work and their level of performance is the way they are treated by their managers. Direct supervisors and senior line managers have the power to make or break levels of employee engagement.

Here, we ask employees what they think about their managers and organisational leaders, how well they perceive their organisation to be performing, how communication is managed, and what opportunity people have for participation and involvement.

'Attitudes towards senior managers are especially negative. This has important implications for engagement, performance and intentions to quit.'

A majority of employees think that their organisation is doing at least as well as other, similar organisations. Unfortunately, our survey finds large numbers of people dissatisfied with their line managers, senior managers and communication within their organisation. This reflects the findings from earlier CIPD studies of employee attitudes. Attitudes towards senior managers are especially negative. This has important implications for engagement, performance and intentions to quit. The core topics examined were:

❖ employees' perceptions of managers

❖ employees' perceptions of organisational leaders

❖ communication

❖ participation

❖ appraisal.

WHAT EMPLOYEES THINK ABOUT THEIR MANAGERS

We asked a series of questions aimed at finding out what people really think about their boss (see Chart 10 on page 14).

The chart shows that although more than half of the sample respond positively to nine out of the twelve statements, a sizeable minority respond negatively. Particularly worrying are the 32% who say that their manager rarely or never discusses their training and development needs, the 30% who say that their manager rarely or never gives them feedback on their performance, and the 25% who say that their manager rarely or never makes them feel their work counts.

These results can be broken down further.

Chart 10 Line manager strengths and weaknesses

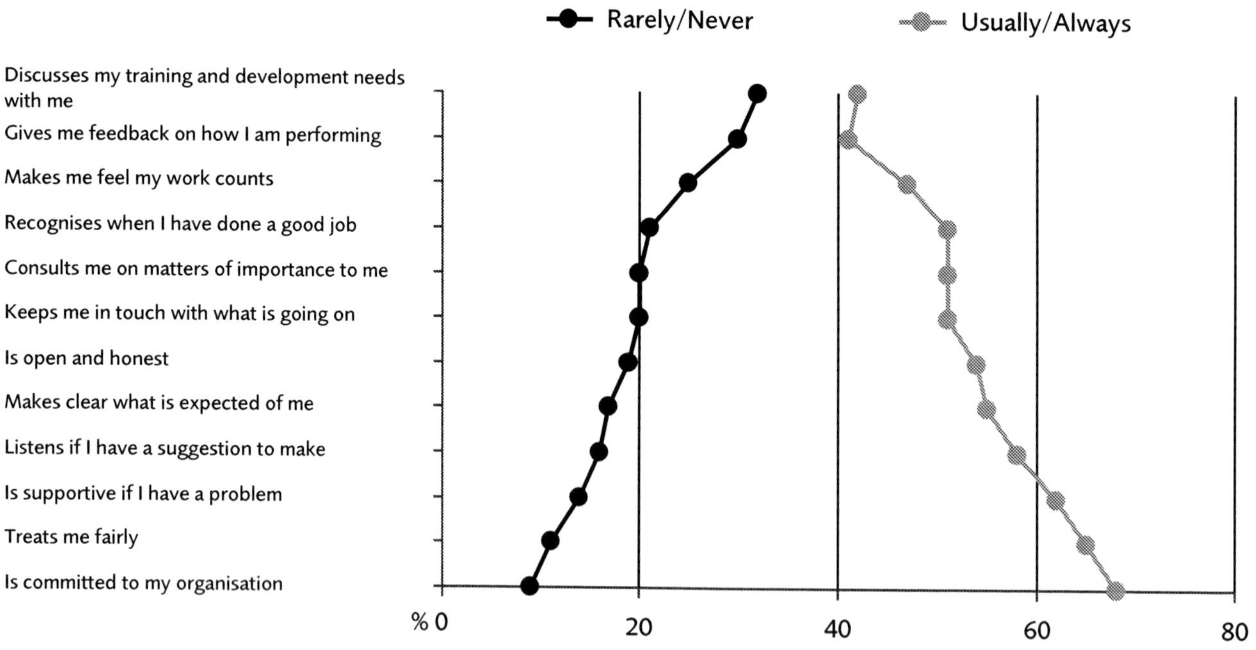
Rarely/Never
Usually/Always
Discusses my training and development needs with me
Gives me feedback on how I am performing
Makes me feel my work counts
Recognises when I have done a good job
Consults me on matters of importance to me
Keeps me in touch with what is going on
Is open and honest
Makes clear what is expected of me
Listens if I have a suggestion to make
Is supportive if I have a problem
Treats me fairly
Is committed to my organisation
% 0
20
40
60
80

Consults me on matters of importance to me

Those on flexible working arrangements are significantly more positive, 59% saying that their manager always or usually consults them, compared with 47% of those not on flexible contracts. More managers (58%) say that they are always or usually consulted, compared with 47% of those with no managerial responsibility. There is no difference in terms of gender, sector or company size.

Discusses my training and development needs with me

More positive	***Less positive***
women	*men*
public sector workers	*private sector workers*
flexible workers	*non-flexible workers*
managers	*non-managers*

Recognises when I have done a good job

Those on flexible contracts are significantly more positive (57%) than those who are not (47%). Managers are much more likely to be recognised for a good job (54% always or usually are recognised) than non-managers are (48%). Employment status, sector and company size do not make a difference. A similar question in the 2004 CIPD Employee Attitude Survey elicited a comparable response overall.

Makes me feel my work counts

Fewer than half of respondents (47%) say that their manager makes them feel their work counts. One quarter (25%) say that they rarely or never do this. While organisational size, sector and gender do not make a difference, those on flexible contracts are significantly more likely to say that they always or usually are made to feel their work counts than those not on flexible contracts. Managers are significantly more positive than non-managers.

> *I'm 58 now and have far more experience than anyone else here. My current general manager semi-jokingly said to me two years ago, 'How old are you now, Steve? Fifty-six? Good God, what are you still doing here? They normally start leaving at fifty.*
>
> Steve, 58, Manager

Gives me feedback on how I am performing

The responses to our survey on the issue of feedback are more negative than those of the previous CIPD Employee Attitude Survey of 2004, where 23% said they rarely or never get feedback on their performance, compared with 30% in this survey. Those on flexible contracts are again more likely than those not on such contracts always or usually to get feedback: 47%, compared with 37%. These relatively low levels of feedback are particularly worrying, as other research has shown that employees need to be told how they are doing in order to be engaged.[1] Gender, age, sector and organisational size do not make a difference.

Is supportive if I have a problem

Those on flexible contracts are significantly more positive than those not on such contracts. Those with a disability are significantly more likely to say their manager is rarely or never supportive than those with no disability: 22% compared with 13%. Managers are significantly more likely to say their boss is supportive than non–managers: 65% compared with 60%.

> 'Managers are significantly more likely to say their boss is supportive than non–managers...'

I've got severe arthritis and I've just had a knee replacement, but they have provided me with some special equipment, a lap-top and a chair at home and at work.

John, 62, Tribunal Member

Keeps me in touch with what is going on

Those on flexible contracts are significantly more positive than those not on this kind of contract. Managers are more positive than non-managers.

Makes clear what is expected of me

Significantly more permanent employees respond negatively to this question than temporary workers, while more employees on flexible contracts respond positively than non-flexible workers.

Listens if I have a suggestion to make

Graduates respond much more positively to this than those with lower-level qualifications. Again, those on flexible contracts are significantly more positive than non-flexible. Employees with a disability are more negative, 23% saying their boss rarely or never listens, compared with 16% of other employees. Managers are more positive than non-managers. As Anne's story on pages 29–30 shows, not being listened to can have very detrimental effects on people's morale.

Treats me fairly

Flexible workers are significantly more positive than those not on flexible contracts. Managers are more positive than non-managers.

Is committed to my organisation

Those on flexible contracts and managers are significantly more positive than non-managers and those not on flexible contracts.

We also asked respondents how confident they are that if they have a problem at work, it will be dealt with fairly. Half of all respondents agree with this, while 18% disagree. Part-timers and temporary workers feel significantly more positive than full-timers and permanent staff. There is no difference between managers and non-managers.

Key findings

❖ One-third of employees report that their line manager rarely or never discusses their training and development needs with them.

❖ Just over half (51%) of employees agree that their manager usually or always consults them on matters of importance to them, recognises when they have done a good job or keeps them in touch with what is going on.

❖ Slightly more (54%) believe that their manager is always or usually open and honest.

❖ Some 41% of employees always or usually get feedback on how they are performing; those who get more feedback also get higher ratings in their appraisal.

❖ Just under half (47%) of employees are always or usually made to feel that their work counts.

❖ Managers and those on flexible contracts generally report more positive responses than non-managers and those on non-flexible contracts.

WHAT EMPLOYEES THINK ABOUT THEIR ORGANISATIONAL LEADERS

We asked people whether senior management have a clear vision of where the organisation is going. Fewer than half of respondents (47%) agree, while a quarter (25%) disagree (see Chart 11). Men, managers and those working in the public sector are significantly more likely to disagree than women, non-managers and private sector workers.

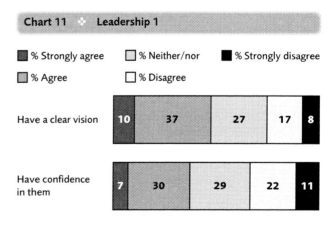

Chart 11 ❖ Leadership 1

■ % Strongly agree □ % Neither/nor ■ % Strongly disagree
▨ % Agree □ % Disagree

Have a clear vision: 10 | 37 | 27 | 17 | 8

Have confidence in them: 7 | 30 | 29 | 22 | 11

Just over one-third of respondents (37%) agree that they have confidence in the senior management team of their organisation, while nearly as many (33%) disagree. Women are significantly more positive than men in response to this question.

MANAGEMENT, LEADERSHIP AND COMMUNICATION

Q: What single change would most improve your working life?

If senior management listened to staff on the ground.

To let senior management know how demoralised the workforce is when constantly threatening large numbers unnecessarily with redundancy when only small numbers are affected.

This is one of the few issues where there is a difference according to age; younger workers in the 16–24 age group are much more likely to agree that they have confidence in their senior managers and directors than do older workers. Full-time workers and those on permanent contracts have significantly more confidence than part-time and temporary workers. Workers in the public sector have less confidence than private sector workers. Those who have worked for their employer for less than 12 months have more confidence than others, which is probably correlated with the younger age groups, suggesting that as employees gain more work experience, they become more cynical about their senior managers.

'...as employees gain more work experience, they become more cynical about their senior managers.'

We also asked respondents whether they trust their senior management team. Just over one-third (34%) agree that they trust their directors or senior management team, whereas 35% disagree (see Chart 12). While 40% of men disagree that they trust their directors, this is true of just 29% of women.

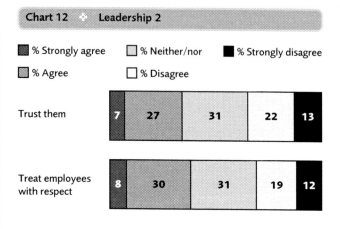

Chart 12 ❖ Leadership 2

■ % Strongly agree □ % Neither/nor ■ % Strongly disagree
▨ % Agree □ % Disagree

Trust them: 7 | 27 | 31 | 22 | 13

Treat employees with respect: 8 | 30 | 31 | 19 | 12

My direct managers, yes, I have confidence in them, but people higher up – you never trust them anyway. They get paid huge amounts of money and push a pen around a piece of paper.

Sally, 32, Administrator

Full-time and permanent workers are significantly more distrustful of their senior management team than part-time and temporary workers. Public sector workers are also more distrustful than private sector workers. Again, those with less than 12 months' service are significantly more trusting than those with longer service.

'Full-time and permanent workers are significantly more distrustful of their senior management team than part-time and temporary workers.'

We also asked whether directors and senior managers treat employees with respect: 38% of respondents agree, while 30% disagree.

More likely to agree	*Less likely to agree*
women	*men*
younger workers 16–24	*older workers*
part-timers	*full-timers*
temporary workers	*permanent workers*
those on flexible contracts	*non-flexible workers*
workers in small organisations	*workers in larger organisations*

Key findings

❖ One quarter of people do not think senior managers have a clear vision of where their organisation is going.

❖ Only 37% have confidence in the senior management team of their organisation.

❖ Only 34% trust their senior managers.

❖ Only 38% think that senior managers treat employees with respect.

❖ Workers in the public sector are more distrustful of senior managers and have less confidence in them than do their private sector counterparts.

❖ Younger people aged 16–24 are significantly more trusting of senior managers than are older workers.

SENIOR MANAGEMENT VISION V INDIVIDUAL SUPPORT TO ACHIEVE OBJECTIVES

By comparing whether employees perceive senior management as having a clear vision as leaders with the extent to which employees feel that they themselves support the achievement of organisational objectives, an interesting profile emerges. Almost two in five employees (38%) can be described as 'Committed Visionaries', who agree that there is clear vision from the top of their organisation and feel inclined to support the achievement of their organisational objectives. This group is more likely than the average to feature private sector workers, and is highly engaged. The next largest group, 'Committed Non-Visionaries' (13%), are committed to helping their organisation achieve its objectives but lack belief in the vision at the top. These are more likely to be men, public sector workers, full-timers and those in managerial positions. A relatively large body of 'Fence-sitters' makes up almost half (43%), and these employees need to be convinced if their potential is to be maximised. In the minority are the 'Blinkered Non-Committers' (4%), who have little belief in senior management's vision and little commitment to achieving its objectives, and the 'Uncommitted Visionaries' (2%), who have bought into the vision but remain uncommitted to assisting the delivery of organisational objectives. (See Chart 13.)

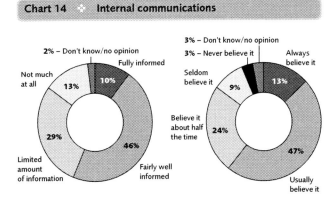

Chart 14 ❖ Internal communications

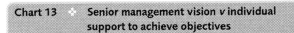

Chart 13 ❖ Senior management vision v individual support to achieve objectives

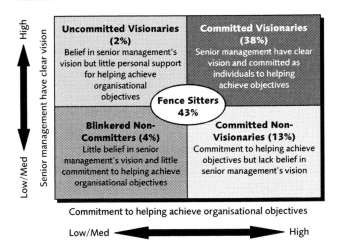

COMMUNICATION

Over two-fifths (42%) of respondents say that they are not kept very well informed about what is going on in their organisation. There are no differences between the public and the private sectors, or in terms of organisational size or job function, although graduates are significantly more likely to say they are kept well informed than others. People on flexible contracts are more likely to say that they are kept well informed than those who are not.

> 'People on flexible contracts are more likely to say that they are kept well informed than those who are not.'

Most respondents say that they can usually believe the information they receive about what is happening in their organisation, but only 13% say they can always believe it, and 12% say that they can seldom or never believe it. (See Charts 14 and 15.) Workers in the private sector are significantly more likely than their public sector counterparts always or usually to believe organisational communication.

Chart 15 ❖ Credibility of information received

% Always/usually believe

62%

■ Public
□ Private

58%

Key findings

❖ Just over half of respondents (56%) feel that they are fully or fairly well kept informed about what is happening in their organisation. This is very important, as our survey shows that this is a major driver of engagement.

❖ Three-fifths (60%) say that they can usually or always believe information they receive about what is happening in their organisation.

Further cross-analysis into the responses on internal communications gives us an interesting perspective.

The level of information that British working adults feel they have is compared against the perceived credibility of the information they receive. In Chart 16 on page 18, the top right quadrant shows that a relative majority (47%) can be described as 'Informed Believers'; that is, they are more likely to know what is happening in their organisation and to feel that the information they receive is credible. This group is of a broadly average profile, with no major differences between sub-groups, but more likely than average to be engaged. In the bottom left quadrant are the 'Uninformed Doubters', who constitute 11%. They receive a low level of information and are less likely to believe it. This group is more likely to be men, public sector workers and full-time workers, and to have low levels of engagement. A further group, the

MANAGEMENT, LEADERSHIP AND COMMUNICATION

'Uninformed Believers' (bottom right), making up 13%, are kept in the dark but do believe the little information they receive. These are more likely to be women, private sector workers and non-managers, all with below-average engagement levels. Finally, the 'Informed Doubters' (top left) are well informed but are likely to doubt communications; fortunately they are just a minority, at 1%. Over a quarter of our sample can be described as 'Fence-sitters', with no strong opinion on the level or credibility of their organisational communications. (See Chart 16.)

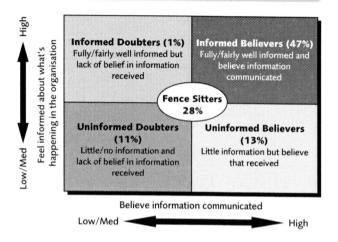

Chart 16 ❖ Level *v* credibility of information

PARTICIPATION

One quarter of respondents say that they are dissatisfied with opportunities in their organisation to feed their views and opinions upwards, while 37% are satisfied (see Chart 17). This does not appear to be influenced by organisational size or sector. However, managers are significantly more satisfied with the opportunities they have than non-managers: 44% compared with 34%.

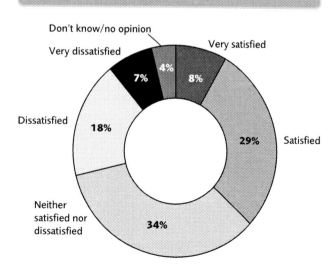

Chart 17 ❖ Satisfaction with opportunities for upward feedback

DOWNWARD *V* UPWARD COMMUNICATION

The level of information that British working adults feel they receive can be compared with the opportunities they perceive they have for upward feedback. The 'Informed Communicators' group (top right quadrant), who constitute 32%, are those who feel informed about what is happening in their organisations and who also feel they have the opportunity for upward feedback. This group is more likely to feature managers and are, not surprisingly, highly engaged. Conversely, 18% can be described as 'Uninformed Non-Communicators'; these have little information or opportunity for upward feedback. Men and full-time workers, who display low levels of engagement, are more likely to feature in this group.

Relative minority groups here are the 'Informed Non-Communicators' (6%), with information but little upward feedback opportunity, and the 'Uninformed Communicators' (5%), who have the chance for upward feedback but little information coming to them. Just under one in four are 'Fence-sitters' and therefore open to persuasion. (See Chart 18.)

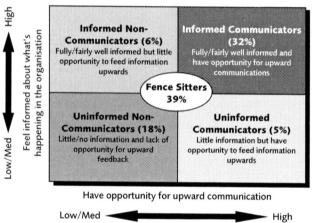

Chart 18 ❖ Downward *v* upward communication

APPRAISAL

Over two-fifths (44%) of employees have not had a performance appraisal in the past year (see Chart 19 opposite). This is particularly true of those in small organisations of fewer than 25 employees, part-time workers and temporary workers. While 65% of managers have had an appraisal, this is true of just 50% of others.

Key finding

❖ People who have more positive perceptions of their leaders and managers and of communications within their organisation are more engaged, receive higher performance ratings, rate themselves as high performers and are less likely to quit.

In addition, people who have a positive view of their managers also have a generally positive set of emotions about their work and

Chart 19 ❖ Performance appraisal in last year

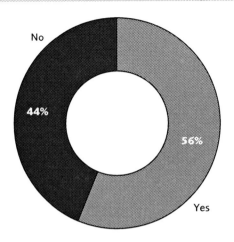

'...people who have a positive attitude towards their workplace may be more likely to be given opportunities that engage them in their work...'

Key findings

❖ Men are less satisfied with their leaders and with communication in their organisation than women.

❖ Public sector employees have more negative perceptions of their leaders than private sector employees.

❖ Managers are less satisfied with their line managers but more satisfied with communication within their organisation than non-managers.

ENDNOTE

1 LUTHANS, F. and PETERSON, S. (2002) Employee engagement and manager self-efficacy. *Journal of Management Development*. Vol 21, No 5/6. pp376–387.

their organisation. However, cause and effect are intertwined. People who succeed in their organisations are likely to see their organisations as good places to work and their managers as effective. Likewise, people who have a positive attitude towards their workplace may be more likely to be given opportunities that engage them in their work and make them want to stay.

ATTITUDES TO WORK

4

❖ **71% of managers, and 57% of non-managers say their work is important to them**

❖ **People derive most of their work satisfaction from their relationship with co-workers**

❖ **Workers on flexible contracts are significantly more satisfied than others**

❖ **Increased autonomy increases control and can reduce work-related stress**

❖ **A quarter of all workers rarely or never look forward to coming to work**

❖ **The greatest degree of loyalty is towards co-workers**

Q: What single change would most improve your working life?

More responsibility.

Fewer tedious work assignments.

To have more work to do; I am often bored because I have little to do.

To have the opportunity for self-development and to feel that my skills are fully utilised.

The opportunity to stretch myself.

Doing work that is more meaningful to me.

> 'The performance of organisations also depends crucially...on how employees respond emotionally to their work.'

Many people spend more of their waking hours at work than with their families. The way we feel when we are at work is therefore an important part of our overall emotional well-being. The performance of organisations also depends crucially not just on people's cognitive input, but on how employees respond emotionally to their work.

In this chapter, we ask: how do people feel about their work? Are they satisfied with the work they do, is their work meaningful to them, are they committed to their organisation? Do they feel stressed and pressured, and if so, what impact does this have on their performance? The core topics examined were:

❖ the meaningfulness of work

❖ job satisfaction

❖ experiences of stress and pressure at work

❖ emotional responses to work

❖ commitment and loyalty.

MEANINGFULNESS

As Elizabeth's story shows (see page 35), whether or not someone's work is personally meaningful to them has a big impact on how they feel about their work overall. People whose work goals are related to their own interests and goals are much more likely to be motivated. In turn, this can lead to higher performance (see Chart 20).

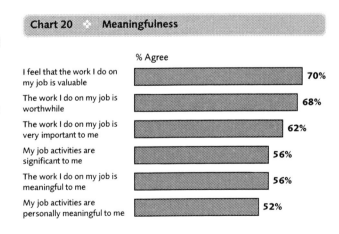

Chart 20 ❖ Meaningfulness

% Agree

I feel that the work I do on my job is valuable	70%
The work I do on my job is worthwhile	68%
The work I do on my job is very important to me	62%
My job activities are significant to me	56%
The work I do on my job is meaningful to me	56%
My job activities are personally meaningful to me	52%

Three-fifths (62%) of those who took part say that their work is very important to them, compared with just 15% who disagree. Permanent workers are more likely to agree than temporary workers, as are those on flexible contracts as opposed to non-flexible workers. One particularly strong finding is the difference between managers and non-managers. While 71% of managers say their work is important to them, this is true of just 57% of non-managers.

Fewer respondents agree that their work activities are personally meaningful to them (just 52%). Chart 21 shows the most significant differences between groups.

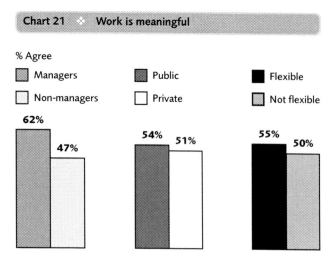

Chart 21 ❖ Work is meaningful

% Agree

▨ Managers ▨ Public ■ Flexible
☐ Non-managers ☐ Private ▧ Not flexible

62% 47% 54% 51% 55% 50%

Traditionally, public sector workers have been regarded as having a distinctive set of values, and this is reflected in our study too. Overall, 68% feel that their work is worthwhile, but this is true of 74% in the public sector, compared with 62% in the private sector. More of those on flexible contracts and managers agree than non-flexible workers and non-managers.

A very high 70% overall feel that the work they do in their job is valuable.

Key findings

❖ Having meaningful work is important to almost all professional groups.

❖ Public sector workers find their jobs more meaningful and worthwhile than do those in the private sector.

❖ Those on flexible contracts find their jobs more important, more worthwhile and more meaningful than do those not on flexible contracts.

Job satisfaction

Employers often want to know how satisfied people are with their job overall. Somewhat disappointingly, we found that, overall, 52% of respondents feel satisfied or very satisfied with their current job, while 26% are dissatisfied. This is more or less in line with findings from other studies. (See Chart 22.)

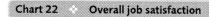

Chart 22 ❖ Overall job satisfaction

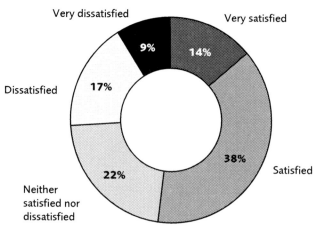

Very dissatisfied 9%   Very satisfied 14%

Dissatisfied 17%

Satisfied 38%

Neither satisfied nor dissatisfied 22%

Although previous research has tended to show that men are more satisfied than women with their job, this is not true of our sample.[1] We found that those who are satisfied with their job overall are also more engaged with their work than others. (See Chart 23.)

Chart 23 ❖ Job satisfaction by group

% Satisfied

▨ Flexible ▨ Disability ■ Managers
☐ Not flexible ☐ No disability ▧ Non-managers

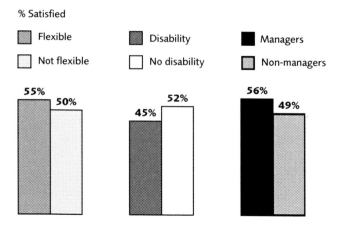

55% 50% 45% 52% 56% 49%

Involvement v job satisfaction

About one-third (34%) of working adults can be described as the 'Enchanted-Involved', that is, they feel interested and involved in their organisations and are satisfied with their current jobs. This group displays high engagement levels and is more likely (but not exclusively) to be found in managerial positions. Conversely, the 'Disenchanted-Uninvolved' – 16% – are those who have little or no interest or desire for involvement and who are dissatisfied in their jobs. This group shows low engagement levels and is more likely to feature men and private sector workers. Of interest is the untapped 'Enchanted-Uninvolved' group (17%), who are happy with their jobs but have a strong desire for greater involvement.

This group has above-average engagement levels, with part-time workers particularly keen for more involvement, as are women and public sector employees. Over one-fifth of employees are 'Fence-sitters' and therefore open to more positive persuasion. One in ten employees can be described as 'Disenchanted-Involved' and are dissatisfied with their jobs, despite feeling involved in their organisation. (See Chart 24.)

> 'Over one-fifth of employees are 'Fence-sitters' and therefore open to more positive persuasion.'

Chart 24 ❖ Involvement v job satisfaction

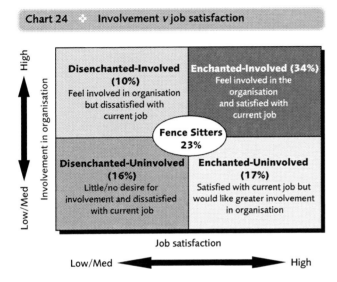

Key finding

❖ Employees who are more satisfied with their work overall are also more engaged.

We have broken this down further to measure levels of satisfaction with particular aspects of work. (See Charts 25–6.)

Chart 25 ❖ Job satisfaction 1

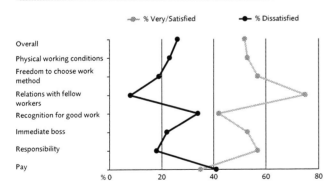

Chart 26 ❖ Job satisfaction 2

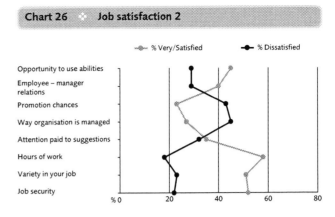

These findings are very important. What we can see here is that people currently derive most of their work satisfaction from their relationship with their fellow workers and are most dissatisfied with the way their organisation is managed, their chances for promotion and their pay.

Almost half of respondents (45%) say that they are dissatisfied with the way their organisation is managed, 43% are dissatisfied with their chances for promotion and 41% are dissatisfied with their pay. Thirty-four per cent are dissatisfied with the recognition they get for good work and 32% are dissatisfied with the attention paid to suggestions they make.

Almost one-third of respondents (29%) are dissatisfied with the opportunity they have at work to use their abilities, suggesting there is huge, untapped potential in the workforce.

We can break these findings down even more by looking at particular groups of workers. A general trend is that employees on some form of flexible contract are significantly more satisfied than others, and this is an important finding which, taken with the findings of earlier chapters, suggests that it is very much in the interests of employers to offer more forms of flexibility. Managers also tend to be more satisfied with most aspects of their work than are non-managers. Workers in the public sector are much less satisfied with the opportunity they have to use their abilities in their work but, conversely, are more satisfied with their hours of work.

Key findings

❖ Just over half of people are satisfied with their job overall.

❖ People derive most satisfaction in their jobs from their relationships with their colleagues.

❖ Twenty-seven per cent are satisfied with the way their organisation is managed.

❖ One in three employees are dissatisfied with the opportunities to use their abilities.

❖ Those on flexible contracts are more satisfied than non-flexible workers.

EXPERIENCES OF STRESS AND PRESSURE

Q: *What single change would most improve your working life?*

Less stress.

More staff – we are currently extremely overworked, with one staff member on long-term sick leave and another having left. Neither has been replaced.

Less stress from customers.

Levels of stress in the workplace are supposedly on the rise. It has been said that nearly 10% of the UK GNP is lost every year as a result of workplace stress.[2] What about our sample? Two-fifths of respondents (40%) say that their job is not at all stressful or only mildly stressful, but 22% report experiencing high levels of stress. (See Charts 27–8.)

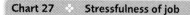
Chart 27 ❖ Stressfulness of job

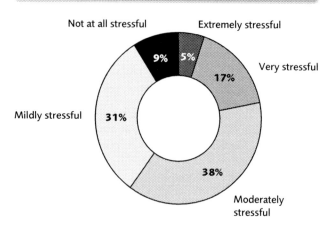

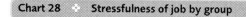
Chart 28 ❖ Stressfulness of job by group

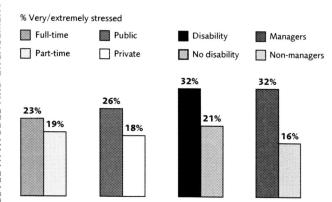

We also asked how often people feel under excessive pressure in their jobs. Some 14% say they 'never' feel this, compared with 15% who feel pressured 'every day'. Overall, 44% of the sample say that they feel under excessive pressure once or twice a week or more, which is a very high level (see Chart 29). We found that those who work longer hours report higher levels of stress than those working shorter hours. Interestingly, there is no relationship between levels of stress and levels of engagement.

> 'Interestingly, there is no relationship between levels of stress and levels of engagement.'

Workers aged 55+ are significantly more likely to experience excessive pressure every day than others, as are those in the public sector, workers with a disability, and managers.

Chart 29 ❖ Excessive pressure in job

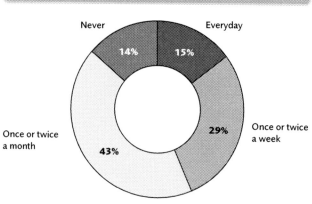

Another important factor is how much control people feel they have over their work. Perceived control has been shown to be a critical psychological construct. People who feel that they are not in control of their work are more likely to experience stress. Increased autonomy increases control and can reduce work-related stress.

Most workers (69%) report feeling a great deal of control or a fair amount of control over they way they do their work, while 11% report having little or no control (see Chart 30). Workers with a disability are significantly more likely to feel that they have little control compared with those without a disability – 18% compared with 10%. Unsurprisingly, non-managers feel they have less control than managers.

Chart 30 ❖ Control over the way job is done

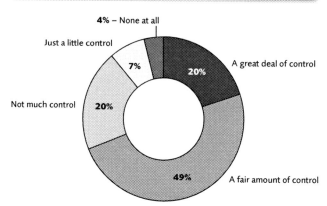

Key findings

❖ Nearly a quarter of employees experience high levels of stress.

❖ Employees who work long hours are more stressed.

❖ Nearly half of employees feel they are under excessive pressure once or twice a week or more.

❖ Older workers, those in the public sector, managers and those with a disability experience more excessive pressure every day than others.

EMOTIONAL RESPONSES TO WORK

Understanding emotions at work is important to understanding people's behaviour and is a critical element in performance management. In many jobs, people who feel positive about what they do are also engaged and able to perform to the best of their ability.

When we asked respondents how often they really look forward to coming to work, only 6% say 'all of the time' (compared with 13% in the 2004 CIPD Employee Attitude Survey), while a further 32% say 'some of the time'; 26% say they rarely or never look forward to coming to work. (See Charts 31–2.)

Chart 31 ❖ Look forward to work

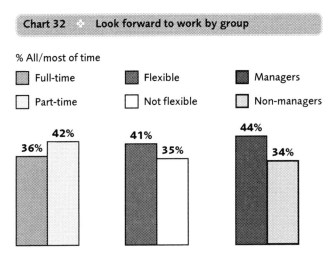

Chart 32 ❖ Look forward to work by group

% All/most of time

Full-time   Flexible   Managers
Part-time   Not flexible   Non-managers

36% 42%   41% 35%   44% 34%

Nearly two-fifths (37%) of respondents say that their work had not, or only occasionally, made them feel enthusiastic over the previous few weeks. This is particularly concerning, given that we found high levels of enthusiasm are associated with high levels of engagement and performance.

While 54% of people report feeling interested and involved in their organisation, a surprisingly high 46% do not feel either interested or involved (see Chart 33).

More interested and involved	*Less interested and involved*
graduates	*others*
those on flexible contracts	*non-flexible workers*
managers	*non-managers*

Chart 33 ❖ Involvement

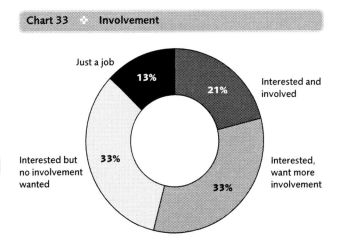

We asked people 12 questions about the emotions that they had experienced over the previous few weeks at work. These items were averaged to create two scales:

1   the extent to which people feel depressed or enthusiastic

2   the extent to which people feel anxious or content.

We found that 33% are content with their work, and 43% enthusiastic about their work.

More anxious and depressed	*Less anxious and depressed*
women	*men*
people being bullied	*people not being bullied*
part-time employees	*full-time employees*
people with disabilities (anxious only)	*people without disabilities*

Interestingly, managers are more enthusiastic, but also more anxious. This may reflect their feelings of responsibility for the work of others.

Key findings

❖ Only 6% of people look forward to coming to work all the time, while 26% rarely or never do.

❖ Nearly half of employees do not feel interested or involved in their organisation.

ORGANISATIONAL COMMITMENT AND LOYALTY

Compared with some of the other findings, those on loyalty are generally very positive. Levels of loyalty are high overall, but there are some interesting differences (see Chart 34).

Chart 34 ❖ Loyalty

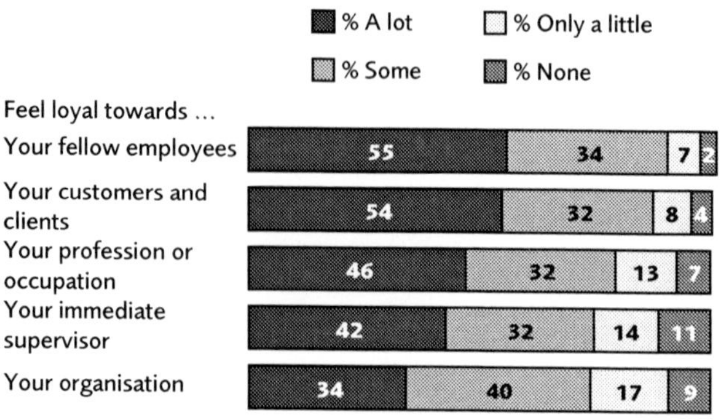

■ % A lot   □ % Only a little
□ % Some   ▨ % None

Feel loyal towards …

	% A lot	% Some	% Only a little	% None
Your fellow employees	55	34	7	2
Your customers and clients	54	32	8	4
Your profession or occupation	46	32	13	7
Your immediate supervisor	42	32	14	11
Your organisation	34	40	17	9

Most respondents (74%) feel some or a great deal of loyalty towards their *organisation*, although this is lower than the 86% recorded in the previous CIPD survey. This is particularly true of flexible workers and managers. Similarly, 70% of people are proud to work for their organisation. Women, those with less than 12 months' service, flexible workers, and managers are especially proud.

Towards their *occupation or profession*, 78% feel some or a great deal of loyalty. Significantly more public sector employees feel a great deal of loyalty towards their profession or occupation than do those in the private sector, 49% compared with 43%.

Loyalty towards occupation or profession

More Loyalty	Less Loyalty
graduates	*non-graduates*
flexible workers	*non-flexible workers*
managers	*non-managers*

Nearly three-quarters (74%) also report some, or a great deal of, loyalty towards their immediate supervisor. This is particularly true of those in very small organisations of fewer than 25 employees, as compared with very large organisations with over 1,000 employees and those on flexible contracts.

Eighty-five per cent report feeling some, or a great deal of, loyalty towards their customers and clients; this is particularly true of women.

The greatest degree of loyalty is towards co-workers: 89% say that they feel some or a great deal of loyalty towards their *fellow employees* – and this is significantly truer of managers than non-managers. This finding is in line with the 2004 CIPD Employee Attitudes Survey.

> *My colleagues are like my family.*
>
> Steve, 58, Manager

> *I think after the TUPE transfer, you have less loyalty to the company. What you have is loyalty to your colleagues.*
>
> Linda, 42, IT Developer

This reflects the findings reported earlier, where more respondents say they are satisfied with their relations with co-workers than with any other aspect of their job.

We asked people whether they felt committed to helping their organisation achieve its objectives and aims: 66% say that they do, only 7% disagreeing (see Chart 35). Managers feel more committed than non-managers: 73% compared with 61%.

Chart 35 ❖ Commitment to helping organisation achieve its aims and objectives

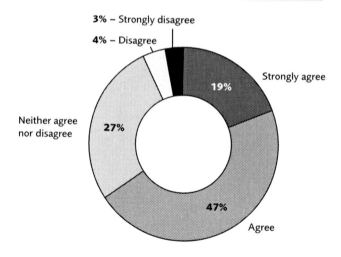

3% – Strongly disagree
4% – Disagree
Strongly agree 19%
Neither agree nor disagree 27%
Agree 47%

Key findings

❖ Three-quarters of respondents feel loyal towards their organisation.

❖ Nearly 90% feel loyal towards their co-workers.

ATTITUDES, DEMOGRAPHICS AND OUTCOMES

Are there differences between men and women, public and private sector workers, and people with or without supervisory responsibility?

Key finding

❖ Women are more satisfied with all aspects of their work than men.

> 'Women are more satisfied with all aspects of their work than men.'

Why is this? There are several possible reasons. One is that more men than women are represented in professional and managerial roles, which may be more stressful than other jobs. Men also tend to be working longer hours than women and to be less satisfied with their work–life balance. Women's expectations of work may be lower than men's if they are juggling multiple roles; however, this may mean that many women are not fulfilling their potential in the workplace.

In Chapter 3, public sector workers' more negative view of their leaders compared with those of private sector employees was revealed. What do they feel about the nature of their work?

Key finding

❖ Public and voluntary workers find their jobs both more meaningful and more stressful than do private sector employees.

This finding is likely to be driven by the nature of the work that people do in the different sectors. It supports previous research in this area that has shown that people who work in public or voluntary sector jobs such as nursing are highly motivated by the nature of

their work and choose to go into jobs that are lower paid than private sector work, but that they consider to be more meaningful.

Key finding

❖ People with supervisory responsibility find their work meaningful and satisfying, are more enthusiastic about their work and committed to their organisations, and experience more job-related stress and anxiety than do people without supervisory responsibility.

These results are driven by three factors:

❖ the characteristics of individuals who want to become managers, such as high levels of enthusiasm for their work

❖ the increased demands of a supervisory role that foster commitment to work and the organisation

❖ the increased stress associated with managerial responsibility.

SIGNIFICANCE OF ATTITUDES TO WORK

The importance of positive attitudes to work has been emphasised throughout this report. Interestingly, evidence from research into emotions at work shows that there are two significant influences on individual emotions: personality and environment, which interact. Some people tend to have a happy outlook on life that is resilient to the stresses of working life. Other people tend to have a negative view even in objectively good circumstances. But most people need organisations to create a positive working environment to sustain their ability to work effectively.

ENDNOTES

1   ARNOLD, J. (2005) *Work psychology*. Harlow: FT Prentice Hall.

2   ARNOLD, J. (2005) *Work psychology*. Harlow: FT Prentice Hall. p389.

ENGAGEMENT

5

❖ **Our study reveals higher levels of engagement than that found in other research**

❖ **Levels of cognitive engagement rise with age**

❖ **Effective individual and organisational management of the relationships and processes that increase positive emotions could raise levels of engagement**

❖ **Over half of respondents say that they exert a great deal of energy performing their job**

It is here that we examine in more detail levels of employee engagement. Engagement is a passion for work. Previous research shows that it has three components:

❖ *cognitive engagement*: focusing very hard on work, thinking about very little else during the working day

❖ *emotional engagement*: being involved emotionally with your work

❖ *physical engagement*: being willing to 'go the extra mile' for your employer and put in work over and beyond contract.

We wanted to know: how engaged are employees with their organisation? To what extent would they recommend their organisation to other people and act as advocates for their employer? Engagement is an interesting concept, because it not only involves how people feel about their work, but also how they behave. The core topics examined were:

❖ overall engagement

❖ cognitive engagement

❖ emotional engagement

❖ physical engagement

❖ advocacy.

> ## Case study
>
> *Anne,* 25, Safety Manager for a pharmaceutical company:*
>
> Anne is contracted to work 40 hours a week but actually works at least 60 hours. She says, 'It just goes with the business. It's a 24-hour business and I do a lot of work for the States, which means that telephone calls are scheduled late in the evening.' Her holiday allowance is 27 days per annum; Anne remarks, 'I'm planning on taking it. If I didn't take holidays, I'd go insane. I don't mind the hours if I take the holiday.'
>
> Generally, Anne is pleased that she is able to work at home two days a week on average. She comments, 'There's no specific policy, but they're pretty relaxed here. The commute is a nightmare, two hours each way, so homeworking is something I asked for. I love it. I find I get a lot more done, although it does tend to mean, because of the commuting, that the rest of the time I find I don't get as much done. So, if anything, I probably work longer hours at home and the days are more effective. It's maybe harder to have a home life and a work life, but even on the days I don't work from home I pretty much always take my laptop home and I'm always working from home. It's the type of business I'm in: my boss is very work-orientated, and the way he does the job means everyone's the same way, really.'

Her long working hours and commute do take their toll on Anne's personal life. She says, 'I've had to put my Master's on hold. I'm supposed to be writing up my thesis and getting it ready for publication. I don't go to the gym as much as I'd like to, and I don't take holidays as much as in the past. I don't have as much time with my family and friends.'

Although Anne enjoys her work, she feels that the way the organisation is managed could be improved. 'There are too many chiefs and not enough Indians. It's a very top-heavy management structure, and there are too many people justifying their jobs without actually getting on and doing it. It's a very patriarchal company, and there are very few women at the top. It's kind of an old boys' network, and that's quite hard to deal with. My manager's not experienced in his role. I like what I do, it's just that the current management could be better. I'm so busy fire-fighting and mopping up the mess from other people I don't have the time to use my technical skills.'

Anne is also concerned about her future career prospects and does not feel that the company offers her any opportunity to progress. She also worries that her manager does not listen to her concerns: 'He can say all the right things but that doesn't work in the long term, because he hasn't actioned anything. I think the people actually having to do the work are very stressed and just have to get on with it. The top dogs have made sure they've looked after themselves, and they couldn't really give a damn about the others.'

Would she recommend her company's products? 'I have to at the minute because I don't have a choice. Really, I think there are other things that do the job just as well.'

*Name changed to protect identity

OVERALL ENGAGEMENT

We found that 35% of employees are actively engaged with their work, 57% are only moderately engaged and 8% are actively disengaged.

Generally, our study reveals higher levels of engagement than has been found in other research; for instance, one study found that 29% of employees are fully engaged in their work, while 54% are not engaged and 17% are actively disengaged.[1]

> '...older employees are more engaged than younger employees...'

Some 37% of women are engaged with their work, and only 6% are disengaged. This is a significantly higher level of engagement than that among men, of whom 34% are engaged with their work and 10% disengaged. Interestingly, older employees are more

engaged than younger employees: 26% of under-34-year-olds are engaged with their work, compared with 41% of those over 35. Unsurprisingly, engagement is also associated with supervisory responsibility: 46% of managers are engaged with their work, whereas 29% of people not supervising anyone are engaged. There are no differences between the public and private sectors.

Key finding

❖ Just over one-third of employees are actively engaged with their work. What is perhaps most worrying for employers is that levels of engagement are much lower among younger workers. This may be due to the kind of jobs they are doing.

COGNITIVE ENGAGEMENT

We asked people four questions to evaluate their level of cognitive engagement in their work. Cognitive engagement means the extent to which people become engrossed in their work. (See Chart 36.)

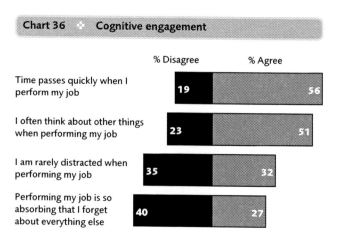

Chart 36 ❖ Cognitive engagement

	% Disagree	% Agree
Time passes quickly when I perform my job	19	56
I often think about other things when performing my job	23	51
I am rarely distracted when performing my job	35	32
Performing my job is so absorbing that I forget about everything else	40	27

Key finding

❖ Some 31% of employees report being cognitively engaged; 22% say they are not cognitively engaged, the lowest level of engagement of the three scales.

However, it also seems that levels of cognitive engagement rise with age: 42% of the 55+ group are engaged cognitively, compared with only 20% of 16–24-year-olds. Managers are more cognitively engaged than non-managers: 39%, compared with 27%. More people with a disability are cognitively engaged than those without, and more people on flexible contracts are cognitively engaged than others (34% compared with 29%).

If we take each dimension in turn, then just over a quarter (27%) agree that they become so absorbed in their work that they forget about everything else, 40% disagreeing.

More absorbed	**Less absorbed**
those on flexible contracts	non-flexible workers
managers	non-managers

More than half of the people surveyed (51%) also say that they often think about other things when performing their job, whereas 23% do not.

Think more about other things	**Think less about other things**
private sector workers	*public sector workers*
non-managers	*managers*

Thirty-two per cent of respondents say that they are rarely distracted when performing their job, compared with 35% who say they are. However, 42% of managers say they are rarely distracted, compared with 27% of other workers.

Finally, more than half of respondents (56%) agree that time passes quickly when they are working, whereas 19% disagree. This is more true of managers than non-managers.

Key finding

❖ Overall, the survey responses reflect an interaction between individual engagement with work and the nature of the work itself. Some jobs are more likely to demand a high level of attention, for example managerial jobs, and they are also likely to attract people interested in cognitively demanding work.

EMOTIONAL ENGAGEMENT

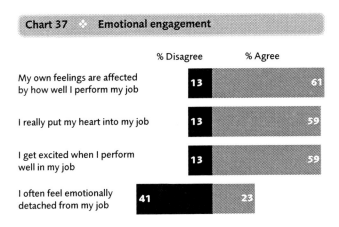

Chart 37 ❖ Emotional engagement

	% Disagree	% Agree
My own feelings are affected by how well I perform my job	13	61
I really put my heart into my job	13	59
I get excited when I perform well in my job	13	59
I often feel emotionally detached from my job	41	23

> 'As is the case with cognitive engagement, emotional engagement increases with age...'

Emotional engagement is concerned with the extent to which people are involved in their jobs at an emotional level. Levels of emotional engagement are higher than those for the other two forms of engagement, 58% of people saying they are emotionally engaged in their work and only 6% saying they are emotionally disengaged. Women are much more emotionally engaged than men (61%, compared with 56%). As is the case with cognitive engagement, emotional engagement increases with age, and managers and those on flexible contracts are more emotionally engaged than non-managers and those not on flexible contracts. (See Chart 37.)

Key finding

❖ Nearly three-fifths (58%) of employees are emotionally engaged with their work.

Turning to the detailed questions, we found that 59% of people say that they 'really put their heart into their jobs', with which only 13% disagree. This is more true of managers, 69% of whom agree, than of non-managers (54%).

The same number overall agree they get excited when they perform well, but there are some differences:

Get more excited when they perform well	**Get less excited**
those on flexible contracts	*non-flexible workers*
managers	*non-managers*

Conversely, we asked whether people feel emotionally detached from their job: 41% overall say that they do not, compared with 23% who do.

Almost two-thirds of respondents (61%) say that their feelings are affected by how well they perform their job, compared with just 13% who say they are not. This is particularly true of private sector workers, graduates, flexible workers and managers.

Key finding

❖ Emotional engagement is closely related to the other aspects of emotions that we have measured in this survey. Feeling emotionally engaged with work runs alongside other positive perceptions of work and the organisational environment, and other aspects of engagement. Effective individual and organisational management of the relationships and processes that increase positive emotions could also raise levels of engagement and performance.

PHYSICAL ENGAGEMENT

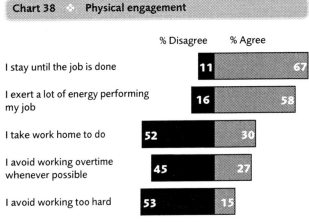

Chart 38 ❖ Physical engagement

	% Disagree	% Agree
I stay until the job is done	11	67
I exert a lot of energy performing my job	16	58
I take work home to do	52	30
I avoid working overtime whenever possible	45	27
I avoid working too hard	53	15

Physical engagement is concerned with how much effort people put into their work. 38% of employees are physically engaged with their work and 11% are disengaged (see Chart 38). Older workers, managers, those with a disability and flexible workers are more engaged than their comparator groups.

Over half of respondents (58%) say that they exert a great deal of energy performing their job; 16% say that they do not. Interestingly, this is more true of part-timers, of whom 63% agree, than full-timers, of whom 56% agree, and is also more true of managers than non-managers.

Key finding

❖ Thirty-eight per cent say that they are physically engaged with their work, with 11% disengaged.

Two-thirds of people (67%) say that they stay until the job is done, compared with 11% who do not. More women than men agree, and 75% of managers agree, compared with 63% of other workers. While 27% say that they actively avoid working overtime, 45% disagree. Managers are significantly more likely to work overtime than non-managers.

> 'Two-thirds of people (67%) say that they stay until the job is done...'

We asked whether employees take work home with them: 30% say they do, compared with 52% who do not.

More likely to take work home	Less likely to take work home
those on flexible contracts	*non-flexible workers*
workers with dependants	*workers without dependants*
managers	*non-managers*

Only 15% of our sample say that they avoid working too hard, while 53% disagree. More men (17%) than women (12%) say that they avoid working too hard, as do workers on a flexible contract. However, although the differences are statistically significant, the numbers are still very small. Sixty per cent of managers disagree, compared with 49% of non-managers.

Key finding

❖ Engagement, performance and intention to stay with the organisation are closely associated. Engaged employees will want to work hard and succeed, and are less likely to want to quit to go and work for another organisation.

ADVOCACY

We asked our respondents whether they would recommend their organisation to someone seeking their advice about a job opportunity. Just over half (52%) agree that they would, 23% saying that they would not (see Chart 39). Interestingly, women and those on flexible contracts are much more likely to recommend their organisation than men and those not on flexible

contracts. Employees with a disability are much less likely to recommend their organisation than those without. (See Chart 40)

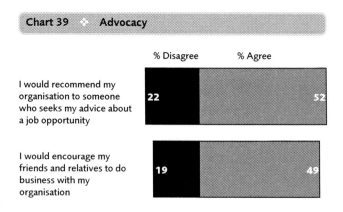

Chart 39 ❖ Advocacy

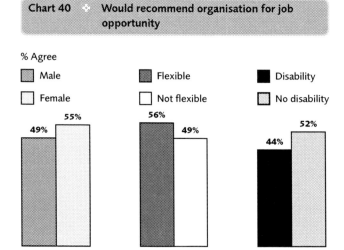

Chart 40 ❖ Would recommend organisation for job opportunity

We also asked whether people would encourage friends and family to do business with their organisation. Fewer than half (49%) say that they would, 19% disagreeing (see Chart 39). Flexible workers are much more positive than those not on flexible contracts (see Chart 40).

We asked people how they would speak of their organisation as an employer to people outside: 50% say they would speak highly of their organisation, while 21% would be actively critical, and 19% would speak highly without being asked. (See Chart 41 opposite.)

More critical	Less critical
men	*women*
full-timers	*part-timers*
public sector workers	*private sector workers*
employees in organisations of 1,000+	*employees in smaller organisations*
workers on non-flexible contracts	*flexible workers*
workers with a disability	*workers without a disability*

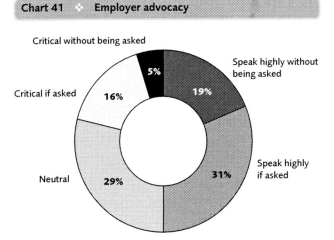

Chart 41 ❖ Employer advocacy

Critical without being asked
5%
Speak highly without being asked 19%
Critical if asked 16%
Neutral 29%
Speak highly if asked 31%

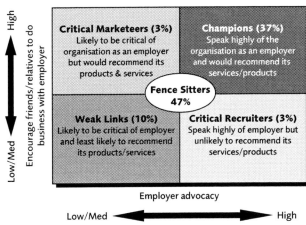

Chart 42 ❖ Employer advocacy v customer advocacy

High ← Low/Med (Encourage friends/relatives to do business with employer)

Critical Marketeers (3%)
Likely to be critical of organisation as an employer but would recommend its products & services

Champions (37%)
Speak highly of the organisation as an employer and would recommend its services/products

Fence Sitters 47%

Weak Links (10%)
Likely to be critical of employer and least likely to recommend its products/services

Critical Recruiters (3%)
Speak highly of employer but unlikely to recommend its services/products

Employer advocacy

Low/Med ←————→ High

Key finding

❖ This survey found that employees who are engaged are also more likely to be positive advocates of their organisation.

EMPLOYER ADVOCACY V CUSTOMER ADVOCACY

Comparing those who speak highly of or who are critical of their organisation as an employer with those who would recommend or would not recommend their organisation's services or products to friends and relatives shows an interesting picture. In the top right quadrant are a powerful group, 'Champions', who make up 37% of the total. This group will willingly promote both their organisation as an employer (potentially reducing recruitment costs) and its services or products (reducing marketing costs), are highly engaged and more likely to be found in the private sector and in managerial positions. Almost half in this case are 'Fence-sitters', with no strong opinions but open to being influenced in a favourable direction. Of concern are the one in ten who can be defined as 'Weak Links': this group has the ability to remove considerable value from their organisation with their negative views of it as an employer and of its service or product offerings. 'Weak Links' display low engagement levels and are more likely to be men, full-time workers and those employed in the public sector. A minority, 3% in each case, are 'Critical Recruiters', who will act as employer advocates but not of its services or products, and 'Critical Marketeers', who are negative about their employer but not of its services or products. (See Chart 42.)

DOES ENGAGEMENT MATTER?

The focus of much of this report has been on the extent to which people are engaged with their work. There are strong associations between all aspects of engagement, people's self-ratings of their performance, their appraisal rating and the likelihood that they will stay with their organisation. These factors are also associated with

loyalty to the organisation and advocating the organisation, that is, speaking highly of the organisation and recommending its products or services to others. In other words, our findings suggest that engagement matters very much and is associated with many other positive aspects of employment from the perspective both of the employee and the employer.

> '...engagement matters very much and is associated with many other positive aspects of employment from the perspective both of the employee and the employer.'

Key findings

❖ Women are more likely to be emotionally and physically engaged with their work, and more likely to speak highly of their organisation, than men. Men are more likely to be loyal to their organisations.

❖ Public and voluntary sector employees are more cognitively engaged with their work, and private sector employees are more likely to speak highly of their organisation.

❖ People with supervisory responsibility are more cognitively and emotionally engaged. People with supervisory responsibility are more physically engaged, more likely to speak highly of their organisation and more loyal to their organisation.

ENDNOTE

1 SEIJTS, G. and CRIM, D. (2006) What engages employees the most or, the ten Cs of employee engagement. *Ivey Business Journal*. Mar–Apr. pp1–5.

OUTCOMES

6

❖ **Some 76% say that their work is excellent, and 82% say that they perform to the best of their ability**

❖ **There seems to be a link between levels of engagement and performance; however, engagement alone is not enough to drive performance**

❖ **To avoid recruitment costs, it would be better to enhance the performance and engagement of disengaged workers, who may otherwise leave**

We need to know what happens as a result of people's experiences at work in terms of whether they intend to quit their organisation, how well they are performing and the levels of sickness absence. Prior research has shown that disaffected employees are more likely to quit and more likely to take sick leave than their more contented counterparts. The core topics examined were:

❖ individual performance

❖ intention to quit

❖ sickness absence.

Case study

Elizabeth,* 60, Part-time Support Worker

Elizabeth is a support worker in a home for adults with severe multiple disabilities. She works two days a week. She feels that her employers are flexible if she needs to change her hours or days of work: 'I've changed my hours three times over the last five years and the firm are flexible. Mostly I think they have a very positive attitude and do try to accommodate people's needs.' She feels that part of the reason for this is that the home is run by a charity. She explains that being able to work flexibly in this way fits in with her caring responsibilities: 'I have eight grandchildren and during the course of the week I will probably mind between three and five of them. School holidays are here so it's likely to be more.' She says, 'I've adjusted my hours to suit what I want to do in my life as I've got older. I decided at one point to cut my hours, and then two of my daughters were struggling

with their childminding and so I cut my hours and went to four days, and then decided to go to two days, which coincided with my daughter having another baby, so it all worked out well, really. I am fortunate in that the department I work for will accommodate people, if they can, rather than lose people that they consider good.'

Elizabeth feels sorry for younger people working for her organisation, however. She comments, that 'one thing we have is that there isn't anywhere else for people to go, so people in their 20s and 30s will leave.'

Overall, Elizabeth feels very positive about her work and her colleagues. 'I love my job. I've been in it nearly 15 years. I was fortunate enough not to work when my children were small, and I was a childminder at one point, and then I got this job. We have a very, very good team, and most of the time we get on remarkably well. You will be given support; for example, one of the girls finished with her long-time boyfriend and was devastated, but the support that the rest of the staff gave her was amazing.'

'Usually stress is caused not so much by the job: it's usually frustration coming from the senior managers. Our Director is quite bad at delegation, and sometimes we don't get the information we need, or suddenly they'll change their mind. When I wanted to reduce my hours, it wasn't a problem with my superior or his superior, but it had to go to the top man, and I was told by my manager's manager that she would have to wait until he was in a good mood to ask him, and, sorry, that wasn't good enough for me.'

Elizabeth derives a great deal of personal satisfaction from her job and the feeling that her contribution matters:

'the work we do is vital not only for the organisation but also for the parents or the carers of the people we work with. The service users need so much help.'

*Name changed to protect identity

More likely to be rated good/excellent	Less likely
women	men
workers 55+	younger workers
workers with no disability	workers with a disability
managers	non-managers

INDIVIDUAL PERFORMANCE

People were asked to rate their performance according to a number of criteria. First, they were asked whether they feel they have the knowledge they need to do their work to a high standard. The vast majority (81%) agree that they do. We then asked whether people feel they have the skills they need to do their jobs and, again, 81% agree. Like Elizabeth, most of our respondents (76%) agree that their work is of excellent quality, and 82% say that they perform to the best of their ability. (See Chart 43.)

Chart 43   Individual performance

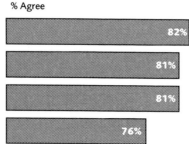

% Agree

Overall, I perform to the best of my ability	82%
I have all the skills necessary to do my job	81%
I have the knowledge that I need to do my work to a high standard	81%
My work is of excellent quality	76%

Of those who have had a performance appraisal, 74% say that they received a rating of 'very good' or 'excellent'. Although the results for all groups are good, there are some differences (see Chart 44).

Chart 44   Performance rating from last appraisal

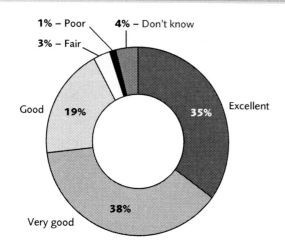

1% – Poor
3% – Fair
4% – Don't know
Good 19%
Excellent 35%
Very good 38%

'Those in the private sector are more likely to say that their performance is higher than that of other people than public sector workers are...'

When we asked people how they think their performance at work compares with others doing a similar job, 54% say they think their performance is higher than others', while just 3% say they think it is lower and 39% say that it is about the same (see Chart 45). The implication of this is that not everyone has an accurate view of their performance. Those in the private sector are more likely to say that their performance is higher than that of other people than public sector workers are, and employees with a disability are significantly more likely to say that their performance is lower than that of others, but numbers are quite small here. On the other hand, 65% of managers say that their performance is higher than that of other people, compared with just 48% of non-managers.

Chart 45   Perceived job performance v others

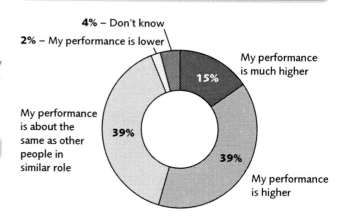

4% – Don't know
2% – My performance is lower
My performance is much higher 15%
My performance is about the same as other people in similar role 39%
My performance is higher 39%

Key findings

❖ The majority of people believe they have the knowledge and skills they need.

❖ Most people think they are performing well and have evidence to support this from their appraisal.

As we have said earlier, there appears to be a link between levels of engagement and performance. This is supported by other studies in this area.[1] However, it would not be true to say that engagement alone is enough. Clearly, people also need to have the right skills and abilities to perform their jobs, as well as the opportunity and the motivation. It is all about creating meaningful jobs for people in an organisational climate with good communication, participatory management styles and plenty of opportunity for people to be involved.

INTENTION TO QUIT

People's expressed intention to leave their organisation is generally regarded as an important measure of how they are feeling about their work. While 47% say that they are either looking around for another job or are in the process of leaving, 53% have either not thought about leaving their job, or have thought about it but not done anything. (See Chart 46.)

Chart 46 ❖ Commitment/intention to leave

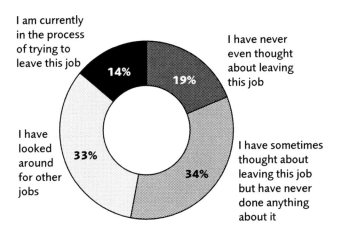

For those intending to leave in the following year, the main reasons given are:

Reason	%
Better pay and benefits	51
Job satisfaction	47
Different type of work	35
Promotion	34
Similar job, different organisation	32
More flexible hours	20

Full-timers are significantly more likely to leave in order to be promoted than part-timers. We found overall that engaged employees are less likely to leave their employer, and more likely to have better levels of performance. On the one hand, this might appear a good thing: disengaged employees who are not performing so well are more likely to quit! However, we have to ask whether it would not, in fact, be better to find ways of enhancing both performance and engagement, rather than take on the cost of hiring new employees. We also need to take into

consideration the potentially detrimental effects that disengaged, low-performing employees may be having on the attitudes, morale and work experiences of their colleagues.

Key findings

❖ Just under a quarter of employees expect to leave within the year.

❖ Thirty-five per cent of people expect to be in the same job the following year.

❖ Nearly half of people are looking for another job.

❖ Although pay and benefits are important reasons for looking for another job, job satisfaction ranks very high.

❖ People who do not feel loyal to their organisation are more likely to want to leave. People who are depressed about their work and dissatisfied with pay and conditions are looking for new jobs, and yet they are still emotionally engaged with their work. Importantly, some of the people looking for new jobs are high-performers in highly skilled occupations.

INTENTION TO QUIT V EMPLOYER ADVOCACY

Comparing employees' intentions to stay or leave their organisation with their propensity to speak highly or be critical of their employer, it is evident that over one-third fall into the desirable 'Apostles' group (top right, Chart 47). These employees are committed to staying with their employers and will speak favourably about them to others. Displaying high engagement levels, these are more likely to be employed in the private sector and in management positions. Almost three in five employees are 'Fence-sitters', and a potentially lucrative group to swing into a more positive position. Just under one in ten fall into the 'Uncommitted Critics' group (bottom left, 9%), intent on jumping ship and taking with them critical views of their employers. In the minority are the Committed Critics (top left, 8%), who are critical but intent on staying, and the 'Uncommitted Apostles' (bottom right, 6%), who will go forth with positive recommendations of their organisations as employers.

Chart 47 ❖ Intention to quit v employer advocacy

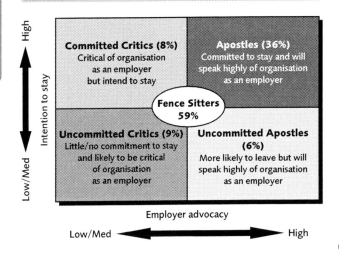

SICKNESS ABSENCE

The majority of workers (82%) take five days or fewer sick leave a year; nearly half (49%) have taken none or only one day in the last year. But, at the other extreme, 5% were off sick for over 20 days. (See Chart 48.)

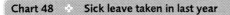

Chart 48   Sick leave taken in last year

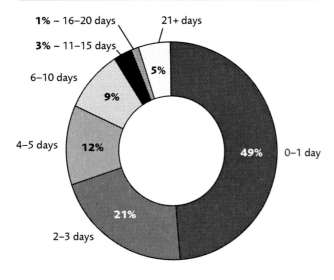

We found some significant differences between different groups of employees concerning sick leave taken. Significantly more men take just 0–1 day's sick leave (53%) compared with 44% of women, but there is no difference between the sexes as regards the likelihood of long-term sick leave of 20+ days. There is also clear statistical evidence that the oldest workers aged 55+ take the least amount of sick leave.

'There is…clear statistical evidence that the oldest workers aged 55+ take the least amount of sick leave.'

Significantly greater numbers of part-time workers take just 0–1 day's sick leave compared with full-time workers (55% compared with 47%), and the same is true of temporary v permanent employees (58% compared with 48%).

Sick-leave levels are significantly higher among public than private sector workers, 22% of the former having taken over five days, compared with 15% in the private sector.

While 19% of employees with a disability had taken over 20 days' sick leave in the previous year, just 4% of those without a disability had. Employees with no children were significantly more likely to take just 0–1 day's sick leave than those with children (51% compared with 45%).

Key findings

❖ Workers aged 55+ take less sick leave than younger employees.

❖ Employees who take more sick leave are less engaged with their work.

❖ There is no association between performance and sickness absence.

ENDNOTE

1 SEIJTS, G. and CRIM, D. (2006) What engages employees the most or, the ten Cs of employee engagement. *Ivey Business Journal.* Mar–Apr. pp1–5.

7

❖ **Allowing people to feed their views and opinions upwards is the single most important driver of engagement**

❖ **The 55+ age group has the strongest set of associations between managerial factors and engagement**

❖ **There is an overall stronger set of associations between managerial factors, engagement and performance for men, suggesting a wider variety of drivers of engagement for women**

❖ **Managers' respectful treatment of colleagues is associated with engagement for people with flexible working arrangements**

The findings of our study have important implications for managers and employers. In this chapter, we consider the overall findings of our survey, and the key actions that managers can take to drive up levels of engagement and performance and improve employees' experiences of their working lives.

MODEL OF ENGAGEMENT

The model in Chart 49 shows the links between managerial behaviour and processes, engagement, performance and intentions to stay with the organisation. The factors included are those that emerged through regression analysis as being the areas

of managerial action most significantly related to engagement levels. However, other aspects of employment, such as job satisfaction, flexibility, age and job content are also strongly associated with engagement. People's levels of engagement need to be considered holistically within the context of managerial actions, features of the job itself and individual preferences.

Six factors should be taken into account when interpreting the model:

1   The managerial factors shown in the overall model are those that are *significantly* associated with engagement, performance and intentions to stay.

Chart 49   ❖   Engagement, performance and retention

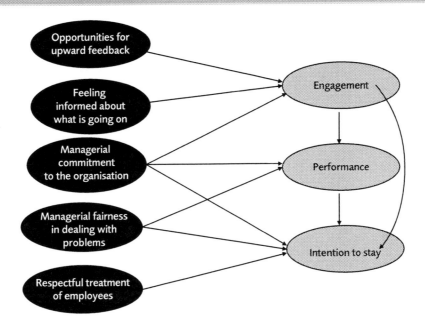

2   In this model, the term 'intention to stay' has been used so that the positive associations between drivers of engagement and performance, and intentions to stay with the organisation are clear.

3   The relationships between the managerial factors and the three individual outcomes (engagement, performance and intentions to stay) are represented by arrows. The arrows show *direct* associations. Some of the factors, notably managerial commitment to the organisation, are associated directly with each of the three individual outcomes. Others, such as opportunities for upward feedback, are directly significant for engagement only. However, this does not mean that opportunities for upward feedback are not important for performance. Rather, opportunities for upward feedback influence engagement, and engagement influences performance. This is an *indirect* association between opportunities for upward feedback and performance.

4   Each of the managerial factors included in the analysis can be considered as the sum of a range of processes and practices. For example, opportunities for upward feedback could encompass communication strategies, organisational culture, and managerial responsiveness to feedback from employees.

5   Opportunities for upward feedback have the strongest association with employee engagement in this overall model.

6   For any individual or organisation, the relationship between managerial processes, engagement and performance will vary. For this reason the associations between the variables are not described numerically: the numbers from analysis of the whole sample would not apply to specific individuals.

Further analysis of the model was carried out to examine differences associated with age, gender, flexible working and sector.

AGE

Participants were grouped into three categories: up to 34, between 35 and 54, and over 55.

❖   There are a number of differences between these age groups in terms of the factors that are associated with engagement and performance. The only common factor across all three age groups is the link between engagement and performance.

❖   For the under-35 age group:

   ❖   Engagement is associated with feeling informed about what is going on in the organisation, and opportunities for upward feedback.

   ❖   Engagement and perceiving organisational commitment in their manager are important to their performance.

   ❖   Managerial fairness and engagement are associated with intentions to stay.

❖   The 35–54 age group data show that:

   ❖   Managers' respectful treatment of colleagues, the organisational commitment of managers and opportunities for upward feedback are related to their engagement.

   ❖   Managerial fairness in dealing with problems and engagement are associated with performance.

   ❖   Perceived managerial commitment is particularly important for intentions to stay in this group.

❖   The over-55 age group has the strongest set of associations between managerial factors and engagement.

   ❖   Feeling informed about what is going on in the organisation and managerial organisational commitment are associated with engagement, and engagement is the key driver of performance.

   ❖   Perceptions that senior managers have a clear vision of where the organisation is going are associated with intentions to stay.

GENDER

❖   The model has an overall stronger set of associations between managerial factors, engagement and performance for men. This suggests that there is a wider variety of drivers of engagement for women than for men.

❖   Managerial commitment to the organisation and opportunities for upward feedback are important to engagement for both men and women.

❖   Managerial commitment and engagement are important to the performance both of men and women.

> 'Managerial commitment and engagement are important to the performance both of men and women.'

❖   Engagement and perceived managerial fairness in dealing with problems are associated with intentions to stay for both groups.

❖   In addition:

   ❖   For men, managers' respectful treatment of colleagues, and feeling informed about what is going on in the organisation are additional factors associated with engagement.

   ❖   For women, confidence that problems at work can be resolved fairly is an additional factor associated with performance.

❖ Managerial commitment to the organisation is related to women's intentions to stay.

FLEXIBLE WORKING

❖ Managerial commitment to the organisation and opportunities for upward feedback are important to engagement for people with and without flexible working arrangements.

❖ Performance in both groups is associated with engagement and perceived managerial commitment to the organisation.

❖ Engagement is associated with intentions to stay for both groups.

❖ In addition:

  ❖ Managers' respectful treatment of colleagues is associated with engagement for people with flexible working arrangements.

  ❖ Fairness in dealing with problems is associated with performance and intentions to stay for this group.

  ❖ Feeling informed about what is going on in the organisation is important for the engagement of people without flexible working arrangements.

  ❖ Intentions to stay are associated with managers' respectful treatment of colleagues, and managerial commitment to the organisation.

MANAGERS AND NON-MANAGERS

❖ There are several differences between managers and non-managers. In general, managers are focused on the behaviour of their peers and leaders.

❖ The vision of senior managers and leaders is important to the engagement of managers.

❖ Perceived managerial fairness in dealing with problems and engagement are significant drivers of managers' performance.

❖ Managerial fairness is also related to managers' intentions to stay with the organisation, as is perceived managerial commitment to the organisation.

❖ Non-managers are more concerned with managerial processes:

  ❖ Managerial commitment to the organisation, feeling fully informed about what is going on in the organisation and opportunities for upward feedback are all significant drivers of engagement.

  ❖ The performance of non-managers is associated with engagement and the perceived commitment of managers to the organisation.

❖ The intentions of non-managers to stay with the organisation are associated with engagement and the perceived fairness of managers in dealing with problems.

SECTOR

❖ Managerial commitment to the organisation is an important driver of engagement for both public and private sector employees.

❖ Managerial commitment to the organisation is also an important driver of engagement for both groups, as is engagement.

❖ Engagement is associated with intentions to stay for employees in both sectors.

❖ In addition:

  ❖ The engagement of public sector employees is influenced by the extent to which senior managers have a clear vision of where the organisation is going.

  ❖ Managerial commitment to the organisation and perceived managerial fairness in dealing with problems are related to intentions to stay in the public sector.

  ❖ Private sector employees' engagement is also associated with feeling informed about what is going on in the organisation, and opportunities for upward feedback.

  ❖ Private sector employees' performance is associated with perceived managerial fairness in dealing with problems.

  ❖ Managers' respectful treatment of colleagues and opportunities for upward feedback are associated with intentions to stay for private sector employees.

KEY MESSAGES

These findings suggest that there is every incentive for managers to consider ways of driving up levels of employee engagement, because these, in turn, will positively affect individual performance. The key messages from the survey are these:

❖ Employee engagement is strongly linked to individual performance levels.

'Allowing people the opportunity to feed their views and opinions upwards is the single most important driver of engagement.'

❖ Allowing people the opportunity to feed their views and opinions upwards is the single most important driver of engagement.

MANAGEMENT IMPLICATIONS

41

❖ Keeping employees informed about what is going on in the organisation is critical.

❖ Employees need to see that managers are committed to the organisation in order to feel engaged.

❖ Having fair and just management processes for dealing with problems is important in driving up levels of performance.

❖ Different groups of employees are influenced by different combinations of factors, and managers need to consider carefully what is most important to their own staff, beyond the more general messages contained in this report.

MANAGEMENT PRIORITIES

In addition to the general issues around engagement, many other points have emerged through the study as being significant for managers. There is much that employers can do to enhance the working experiences of their staff, as well as to enhance levels of engagement and performance.

Working life

Working conditions have important effects on levels of engagement, performance and intentions to quit. Managers can work to create a more positive environment where employees can flourish.

❖ They can create opportunities for people to work flexibly, as this will raise levels of engagement, satisfaction and advocacy, and improve retention rates; those with a good work–life balance are more engaged.

❖ They can allow employees a degree of choice in terms of how they manage their work–life balance, as this is important to individual well-being.

❖ Work–life balance is important for *all* employees, including those who are often neglected in discussions over this issue, such as men, managers and those with a disability. Long working hours are detrimental to health and do not lead to higher levels of performance.

❖ Dissatisfaction with pay will often lead people to quit; a sound pay policy, including benchmarking surveys, is therefore critical to the retention of top performers.

> 'More important than pay is whether or not the content of the job is meaningful to the individual; this is true of all forms of work.'

❖ More important than pay is whether or not the content of the job is meaningful to the individual; this is true of all forms of work. Managers need to give careful thought to how jobs are structured, job content and the working environment in order to create meaningful work for everyone, leading to higher levels of engagement and performance.

❖ Bullying and harassment are worryingly prevalent in the workplace, leading to poor performance, negative psychological states and high intention to quit; there is therefore an urgent need to address the human and systemic failures that may foster a climate where bullying is acceptable.

Management, leadership and communication

❖ The lack of attention paid by managers to employees' training and development needs is likely to be detrimental to longer-term organisational and individual performance.

❖ Employees need feedback on their performance on a regular basis if they are to understand what is expected of them and how to improve.

❖ People need to feel that their work counts in order to perform well.

❖ The ability to consult and involve are critical managerial skills that require more development for a substantial proportion of managers; 18% of employees were found to be 'Uninformed Non-Communicators', receiving little or no information about what is happening in their organisation, and lacking the opportunity for feeding their views upwards.

❖ The management of non-managers appears to be weaker than the management of managers, suggesting that management skills among first-line supervisors are in particular need of being strengthened.

❖ Those on flexible contracts feel much more positive about their line managers than do non-flexible workers, most probably because managers who take the trouble to find ways of helping their staff manage their work–life balance are also those who have better general management skills.

❖ A significant minority of people have a very low opinion of their senior managers and perceive them as untrustworthy; this is likely to be related to visibility, communication and involvement in the workplace, and there is an opportunity here for senior management teams to make a real difference to people's working lives and to organisational performance by strengthening employee involvement practices.

❖ A large number also see senior managers as lacking in vision; only 38% can be described as 'Committed Visionaries', both believing that senior managers have a clear vision and being committed themselves as non-managers to help achieve these objectives.

❖ This suggests that there may be problems of strategy in many organisations and in the communication of strategic vision. It may be more difficult for employees to feel engaged with their work when they do not have a clear understanding of what it is their organisation is trying to achieve.

❖ As nearly half of employees feel they are not well informed about what is going on, organisations need to review their internal communications strategies.

❖ The relatively high level of distrust of senior managers in the public sector is worrying, and may well reflect the amount of change that has affected huge swathes of public sector employees in the UK; senior managers in this sector need to give especial consideration to rectifying this situation.

Attitudes to work

❖ People take their work very seriously and, for the majority of people, their work is very important to them. Just over half of people are doing jobs that are personally meaningful, and they are more engaged than others. Managers need to think carefully about the person–job fit when selecting staff, and develop creative ways to make work meaningful.

> 'People who feel positively about their work also tend to feel positively about their organisation and are more engaged.'

❖ People who feel positively about their work also tend to feel positively about their organisation and are more engaged. This creates a virtuous circle that managers can foster.

❖ Some 17% of employees are 'Enchanted-Uninvolved', satisfied with their current job but looking for greater involvement in their organisation. They represent a significant untapped resource.

❖ Almost half of employees are dissatisfied with the way their organisation is managed; this is an area where managers can usefully deploy their skills to bring about improvements.

❖ Over a quarter (29%) of people are dissatisfied with the opportunities they have to use their abilities, suggesting that managers are missing out on the chance to enhance organisational performance and create jobs that people enjoy.

❖ Nearly a quarter of people feel their job is very stressful, and nearly half say that they feel under excessive pressure on a frequent basis, which is detrimental to individual and organisational health. Personal appraisals offer managers the opportunity not just to tell employees how they are performing, but to find out how they feel about levels of stress in their job.

❖ About a quarter (26%) of people rarely or never look forward to coming to work. As we spend so much of our lives in the workplace, this finding is quite disturbing. Work can be fun, challenging, stimulating, exciting and rewarding for people in all kinds of occupations, leading to employees actually enjoying being at work, rather than regarding it as a painful necessity.

❖ The high degree of loyalty that people feel not just towards their fellow workers but also towards their employers is a cause for optimism. This represents a solid foundation on which to build.

Engagement

❖ We found that levels of engagement are higher than some other studies have suggested. However, it remains true that 35% of employees are actively engaged with their work. Positive associations between engagement, advocacy, performance and intention to quit mean that it is in employers' interests to drive up levels of engagement among their workforce.

❖ Levels of engagement appear to have significant benefits for employees as well, since engagement is positively associated with job satisfaction and experiences of employment. It is therefore in the interests of employees to work for organisations that positively seek to raise levels of engagement.

❖ Organisations that foster high levels of engagement are more likely to retain high-performing employees.

❖ The fact that younger employees are more disengaged than their older colleagues suggests that organisations are failing to meet the needs of younger workers. This is a finding that has potentially serious long-term consequences for organisations and for the career development of young people, and is an area that merits further research.

❖ One-tenth of employees can be described as 'Weak Links', likely to be both critical of their organisation as an employer and unlikely to recommend its products and services, while only 37% are 'Champions', scoring positively along both dimensions. This suggests that there is scope for considerable improvement in levels of advocacy in organisations by driving up scores on those factors with the greatest leverage on advocacy.

Outcomes

❖ The fact that most people feel they have the skills and knowledge needed to do their jobs is encouraging, and suggests that employers are giving employees the capabilities they need. However, the fact that many do not feel satisfied with the opportunities they are given to use their abilities suggests that some are overqualified for the jobs they are currently doing, or that they are not reaching their full potential.

> '...today's good performers could become tomorrow's disengaged workers.'

❖ The vast majority of employees appear to be performing well, which is also very encouraging; however, only just over a quarter are satisfied with their chances for promotion, which suggests that today's good performers could become tomorrow's disengaged workers.

❖ Nearly half of all employees are either looking around for another job or are in the process of leaving; this is an extremely high number, and suggests that engaged, as well

MANAGEMENT IMPLICATIONS

43

as disengaged, employees are looking for another job. Pay and job satisfaction are the main reasons. Employers need to look proactively at ways of increasing retention rates.

❖ The fact that workers aged 55+ take less sick leave than younger workers runs counter to the popular image of older workers as less reliable. Older workers are also more engaged than younger workers. Given demographic trends and the increasing average age of the workforce, these findings provide encouragement for employers to ensure they foster the enthusiasm, capabilities and dedication of older members of staff.

CONCLUSIONS

8

Our survey has revealed a complex, fascinating and, occasionally, surprising picture of working life and attitudes in modern Britain. Like Anne and Elizabeth in our case studies (see pages 29 and 35), most people's attitudes towards their work are influenced by a whole range of factors to do with their personal circumstances, occupation, working conditions, management and leadership, career prospects and so on. The precise mix will differ for each individual. However, our study has clearly shown that the way in which people are managed and led is a critical influence on levels of engagement and, ultimately, performance.

It is very disappointing, although perhaps not altogether unexpected, to find that so many people do not really enjoy going to work and derive relatively little satisfaction from their jobs. In general, employees' views about their managers, senior managers and organisational communication are very negative indeed. Instances of bullying and harassment in the workplace are all too common, leading to low levels of satisfaction, engagement and a high likelihood of quitting for some.

Our study has borne out the theory that high levels of engagement are very important in the workplace. Engagement was found to be positively associated with a range of other attitudes such as job satisfaction, as well as higher levels of performance, advocacy and lower intention to quit. Those who are less engaged with their work tend to take more sick leave, are more likely to quit and tend not to perform so well as their colleagues. This suggests that engagement with work is important for both organisations and individuals.

Although our study found relatively high levels of engagement compared with earlier research, it is nevertheless true that only 35% of those surveyed say that they are actively engaged. A small minority is actively disengaged. Of particular concern is the fact that younger employees are much less engaged than their older

co-workers: only 26% of under-34-year-olds say that they are actively engaged, compared with 41% of those 35+.

We found that the main factors that influence employee engagement are:

❖ having opportunities to feed your views upwards

❖ feeling well-informed about what is happening in the organisation

❖ thinking that your manager is committed to your organisation.

> '...good, sound management practice and jobs that enable employees to fulfil their potential will lead to higher levels of employee engagement.'

Basically, good, sound management practice and jobs that enable employees to fulfil their potential will lead to higher levels of employee engagement. We found that those who are most engaged are also the best performers, people any organisation would like to employ. Ensuring that these employees are nurtured and valued will help to ensure they stay with you, rather than move to your competitor.

Our survey has enabled us to look in some detail at groups of employees, and this has revealed some interesting differences. However, demographic variables should *not* be seen in isolation as predictors of performance or engagement; what we have found is that good management practice and a conducive working environment can lead to high levels of engagement and performance among all groups of workers.

GENDER

Women are, in general, more engaged with their work than men, but they also tend to be doing different kinds of jobs. Women are found predominantly in administration, personal services and retail, whereas more men are represented in the managerial, professional and skilled trades categories. Men tend to work longer hours than women. More women surveyed are happy with their work–life balance than men, and they feel that they get more help from their organisation to achieve this. However, they also experience more bullying and harassment in the workplace and tend to experience higher levels of anxiety. Despite this, women are generally more satisfied with their work and hold more positive views of their senior management team than do men. They are more loyal to their organisation, more likely to recommend their organisation as an employer and report higher levels of loyalty to their customers and clients than men. Interestingly, more women than men report having been rated good or excellent in their performance appraisal.

AGE

We found that workers aged 55+ are more engaged with their work than younger employees, and they are also happier with their work–life balance, working shorter hours than others. They are more likely to have been rated good or excellent in their appraisal and take significantly less sick leave than their younger colleagues. Despite this, the same age group reports experiencing more excessive pressure every day than all other age groups. Interestingly, younger workers aged 16–24 have much more confidence in their senior management team than all older workers, and also are more likely to agree that they treat employees with respect, suggesting that, as they gain more experience in the workplace, people become more cynical. Employees aged under 35 are significantly less engaged with their work than older workers. More research is needed to find out precisely why this is the case. It may be that younger workers are not in occupations that they intend to pursue as a career, or that they are in junior-level jobs. Perhaps levels of engagement rise naturally over time as we get older and as levels of achievement and responsibility increase.

DISABILITY

Employees with a disability tend to work a shorter week but to be less happy with their work–life balance. They experience more bullying and harassment than others and feel less supported if they have a problem. They are also more likely to say that they are not listened to, are less satisfied with their work, and are more stressed and pressured than others. They also feel less control over their work and report being more anxious. They are more critical of their organisation than others. They are less likely to have been rated good or excellent in their performance appraisal and less likely than employees without a disability to remain in their job. Employees with a disability rate their own performance as low compared with those without a disability and also report higher instances of long periods of sick leave. However, we need to bear in mind that 'disability' covers a very broad range of

conditions and also that those with a disability are likely to be experiencing sub-optimal working conditions and to be in jobs that do not match their abilities. These findings are quite concerning, and more research is needed into the employment experiences of people with disabilities to find out how their working lives can be enhanced.

MANAGERS

'Managers find their work more important and more meaningful than non-managers do.'

There are a large number of differences between those who have some supervisory responsibilities and those who do not. Managers work longer hours and tend to take less holiday. They also feel less happy about their work–life balance but earn more than non-managers. Their responses on communication and involvement are much more positive than those of non-managers, and managers clearly feel that they have more support and recognition and are listened to more than non-managers are. More managers have had an appraisal during the past year than other employees and are more likely to report that they are treated fairly at work. However, they are less likely to think that senior managers have a vision. Managers find their work more important and more meaningful than non-managers do. Overall, they are more satisfied with their work, but they are also more stressed and anxious. They report more loyalty to their organisation than non-managers and are more likely to look forward to coming to work. They are also significantly more engaged with their work than non-managers. Managers report higher appraisal ratings than non-managers, as well as higher self-ratings of performance. They say they are less likely to leave their organisation than non-managers and also are more hopeful of promotion.

WORKERS ON FLEXIBLE CONTRACTS

We found some surprisingly strong differences between those working on a flexible contract and other workers across a broad range of issues. Those on flexible contracts tend to be more emotionally engaged, more satisfied with their work, more likely to speak positively about their organisation and less likely to quit than those not employed on flexible contracts. However, there are no differences in terms of performance. Those on flexible contracts, perhaps unsurprisingly, tend to feel that they get help from their employer in managing their work–life balance. However, they also have much more positive views about their immediate manager than those not on flexible contracts and are more loyal to their organisation, as well as more likely to act as organisational advocates. Those working flexibly are more likely to report that their work is important and meaningful to them than those not on flexible contracts. They feel that they are treated more fairly and are listened to more than other workers, and they are also more likely to take part in discussions about their training and development needs. Flexible workers are more likely to stay with their employer and to expect to be promoted.

SECTOR

We found no differences between the public and the private sectors in terms of hours worked; however, public sector workers are more likely to receive some compensation for working extra hours than those in the private sector. We would have expected that public sector workers would be receiving more help from their employer to achieve a good work–life balance, but actually there is no difference. Public sector workers report more bullying and harassment than those in the private sector, are less satisfied with the opportunities they have to use their abilities, are more stressed and pressured and are more critical of their organisation than those in the private sector. They are more likely not to feel their senior managers have a clear vision for the organisation and have less trust and confidence in their senior managers. They are also less likely to believe organisational communication. However, the public sector ethos is reflected in the fact that more public sector workers find their work worthwhile and personally meaningful. Public sector workers rate their own performance lower than private sector employees and are more likely to have taken more sick leave.

'It is worrying that so few employees report feeling actively engaged with their work or satisfied with their job.'

The results of this survey provide employers with a national benchmark against which to evaluate levels of engagement within their own organisation. It is worrying that so few employees report feeling actively engaged with their work or satisfied with their job. The impact of poor management practice, particularly where people feel that they are not kept in touch with what is happening, that they are not able to voice their views and that they do not feel that their problems will be dealt with fairly, should not be underestimated. Where employees feel like this, they will not be engaged with their work, will feel dissatisfied with their job, be less likely to speak highly of their employer and be more likely to quit. There is much that organisations can do to remedy this, and we hope that the findings of this survey will provide employers with the information they need to focus on raising levels of employee engagement across the UK.

TECHNICAL APPENDIX

PARTICIPANTS

The participants in this study were 2,001 adults working in Great Britain. The research sample was organised to reflect the general population with respect to age, gender and working status (part-time or full-time), based on the latest British Labour Force statistics. Ethnicity and geographical region were closely monitored during the fieldwork period to ensure that the profile of respondents was broadly in line with the national profile. Table 5 shows a breakdown of the sample by age, gender and working status.

Table 6 on pages 50-51 gives more detailed information about the sample.

MEASURES

The items in the questionnaire were derived from four sources:

❖ the previous CIPD employee attitude survey, *Employee Well-being and the Psychological Contract* (2004)

❖ Kingston Business School

❖ Ipsos MORI

❖ academic research sourced by the Kingston Business School research team.

Table 5 ❖ Sample information				
	Target		Achieved	
Total	2,000	%	2,001	%
Gender				
Male	1,076	53.8%	1,105	55.2%
Female	924	46.2%	896	44.8%
Working status				
Full-time	1,480	74.0%	1,517	75.8%
Part-time	520	26.0%	484	24.2%
Total	2,000	100.0%	2,001	100.0%
Age				
16–24	282	14.1%	297	14.8%
25–34	438	21.9%	458	22.9%
35–44	526	26.3%	531	26.5%
45–54	438	21.9%	452	22.6%
55–64	278	13.9%	250	12.5%
65+	40	2.0%	13	0.6%

Table 6 ❖ Sample characteristics

Gender	%
Male	55
Female	45

Age Group	%
16–24	15
25–34	23
35–44	27
45–54	23
55+	13

Sector	%
Private sector	54
Public sector	44
Voluntary sector	2

Organisation size	Local office/branch %
Fewer than 10 employees	8
10–24 employees	17
25–99 employees	24
100–499 employees	28
500–999 employees	8
1,000 or more employees	16

Organisation size	Company/organisation %
Fewer than 10 employees	n/a
10–24 employees	9
25–99 employees	13
100–499 employees	15
500–999 employees	10
1,000 or more employees	52

Ethnicity	%
White	91
Mixed	1
Asian or Asian British	5
Black or Black British	1
Other ethnic group	2

Region of residence	%
North East	5
Yorkshire and Humber	10
East Midlands	7
Eastern	6
Greater London	15
South East	19
South West	5
West Midlands	6
North West	10
Wales	5
Scotland	12

Work status	%
Full-time (ie, 30 or more hours per week)	76
Part-time (ie, under 30 hours per week)	24

Table 6 ❖ Sample characteristics (cont)

Educational qualifications	%
Degree or degree equivalent, and above	42
Other higher education below degree level	15
A Levels, vocational level 3 and equivalents	17
GCSE/O Level Grade A*–C, NVQ Level 2 and equivalents	19
Qualifications at NVQ Level 1 and below	2
Other qualifications (including foreign qualifications)	3
No qualifications	3

Children (school age or under)	%
Yes	31
No	69

Marital status	%
Single	30
Married/co-habiting	61
Separated or divorced	8
Widowed	1
Other	<1

Disability	%
Yes	7
No	93

Employment contract	%
Permanent	85
Temporary/fixed-term	15

Manager	%
Yes	36
No	64

Length of service in current employment	%
< 12 months	14
1 up to 2 years	13
2 up to 5 years	27
5 up to 10 years	21
10 years or more	26

Two types of item were used in the survey. The first requested information about the individual respondent, for example age, gender and the length of service in their current organisation. The second type of item asked respondents how they *think* or *feel* about an issue. Each of these items was of the same type, a Likert scale. This gives respondents the opportunity to choose one outcome from of a range of five. For example:

Please tell us the extent to which you agree or disagree with each of the following statements:

The work I do on my job is very important to me

> *Strongly disagree*
>
> *Disagree*
>
> *Neither disagree nor agree*
>
> *Agree*
>
> *Strongly agree*

Each response is scored in the following way:

Response	Score
Strongly disagree	*1*
Disagree	*2*
Neither disagree nor agree	*3*
Agree	*4*
Strongly agree	*5*

The score is stored in the database to be used in analysis.

A number of the factors that were measured in the questionnaire, for example employee engagement, are not easily assessed by one item. A more effective way to measure employee engagement is to use a set of items and take the average score for each person, that is, the total score for that person divided by the total number of items.

For example, the question below asks about two aspects of work–life balance:

Thinking about the balance between your work life and your home life, to what extent do you agree or disagree with each of the following?

> *Strongly disagree*
>
> *Disagree*
>
> *Neither agree nor disagree*
>
> *Agree*
>
> *Strongly agree*

a) *I achieve the correct balance between my home and work lives*

b) *My organisation provides support to help me manage my work–life balance*

A survey participant responds 'strongly agree' to question (a) and 'agree' to (b). This gives them a score of 5 + 4 = 9. Their average score is the sum of the scores on the two items (4 + 5 = 9) divided by the number of items (2) = 4.5. The 4.5 value is that person's *scale score*. This process is used to create *composite scales* that have a scale score for each individual respondent. Each composite scale and its derivation are described below.

Scales sourced by Kingston Business School

Five scales were sourced from academic research by the Kingston Business School research team.

Engagement scales

Engagement is a general passion for work. It was assessed using 13 items from an academic source.[1] Engagement comprises three subcomponents, each of which is measured using a subset of the 13 items:

> Cognitive engagement (4 questions)
>
> Emotional engagement (4 questions)
>
> Physical engagement (5 questions)

The three scales were used both separately, to examine associations between other aspects of people's feelings and perceptions, and together to provide an overall assessment of engagement.

Meaningfulness scale

The meaningfulness scale was derived from the same source as the engagement items. This scale uses six items to assess the degree to which people find their work worthwhile, significant, valuable and meaningful.

Job satisfaction scale

Job satisfaction comprises two elements:

❖ Intrinsic satisfaction, that is, satisfaction with such aspects of work as the opportunity to use your abilities

❖ Extrinsic satisfaction, that is, satisfaction with such aspects of work as pay

The scale was developed in previous research[2] and has been applied widely in a range of organisations. The subscales were used both separately, to provide information about intrinsic and extrinsic satisfaction, and together, to give an overall measure of job satisfaction.

Job-related well-being scales

The job-related well-being scales[3] measured two aspects of emotions experienced in the past few weeks at work:

❖ anxiety – contentment (6 items)

❖ depression – enthusiasm (6 items).

Self-rating of performance scale

The four-item self-rating of performance scale was developed by Kingston Business School researchers adapted from the academic literature.

Scales from Ipsos MORI research

The Ipsos MORI '*Insight*' database was used to provide four sets of scale items relevant to this survey. '*Insight*' is an extensive database of employee research surveys derived from a wide range of sectors and is used to benchmark the performance of employee attitudes. The data are based on a rolling average of scores from many surveys of employees conducted on behalf of Ipsos MORI clients. The current dataset includes around 250 studies carried out by Ipsos MORI (formerly MORI) over the last five years, covering in excess of 2 million British employees.

Perceptions of senior managers

We asked respondents for their views on four aspects of their senior management, for example, whether senior managers have a clear vision of where the organisation is going.

Perceptions of line managers

Twelve items were used to measure perceptions of line managers, for example, recognition for good work and commitment to the organisation.

Organisational communication

Three items assessed the perceived quality and trustworthiness of organisational communication.

Work–life balance

Two items measured respondents' views of the balance between their work and home life, and whether they received organisational support to manage this balance.

Advocacy

Three items asked participants about the extent to which they would speak positively about their organisation, and whether they would recommend their organisation's products and services to others.

Stress

The extent to which people experience stress and perceived lack of control over their work were measured in three items.

Method

An online version of the survey was created by the Ipsos MORI team on a secure Ipsos MORI server, with fieldwork conducted between 5 and 10 July 2006. The survey was designed to start with screening questions to ensure that the respondents were all working adults, and that the sample would reflect the working population in terms of age, gender and working status as based upon British Labour Force statistics. People who did not fit the criteria, for example because they were under 16, were thanked for their interest and the survey was discontinued. Similarly, towards the late stages of fieldwork, the survey was closed to some respondents when the quotas for each of the three criteria were reached.

The sample was derived from ipoints, a marketing database provider. The ipoints service was chosen because it could ensure that a sample of respondents mirroring the working population as a whole would take part. It was also an extremely rapid and cost-effective method for surveying 2,000 people within five working days. Members of the ipoints database were invited by email to participate, and the email provided a clickable link to the survey. Batches of emails were sent out to potential respondents from the ipoints database until all the quotas had been reached. Responses to all items were uploaded to an Ipsos MORI database.

The resulting data were processed and checked by Ipsos MORI in line with strict industry quality standards. The percentage age responses for each question are available from the CIPD website.

DATA ANALYSIS

Cross-tabulations

Cross-tabulations are used to segment a dataset so that differences between subgroups can be examined. For example, the number of men and women in each of the public and private sectors.

Comparisons can then be made to see whether there are important differences, such as whether there are relatively fewer women in the private sector than the public sector. The frequency data for each column in the cross-tabulations were examined to see whether the differences between each group were *statistically significant*. Differences in results for any two groups can be:

1 real differences, that are unlikely to have occurred by chance

2 differences that have occurred by chance

3 small differences or no differences at all.

Statistical testing enables researchers to examine for real, or statistically significant, differences between groups. As a guide, please note that results for different subgroups generally need to differ by a certain number of percentage points for the difference to be statistically significant, although this will depend on the size of the subgroup sample and the percentage finding itself. The tests were performed with a 5% significance level, which means that 95% of the time when we find a significant difference there is an actual difference in the population. Where differences between two groups are reported, this is because we found them to be significant in this way.

Correlation analysis

Correlation analyses were used to examine the strength and direction of association between two variables. For example, age and engagement are significantly and positively associated, engagement increasing with age. However, age and satisfaction with the way work is managed are negatively associated; younger people reported significantly greater levels of this aspect of job satisfaction.

This method of analysis is used throughout this report. Non-significant findings are also reported in places when an expected association was not verified by the data.

Regression analysis

Another form of analysis used was regression analysis. This enabled us to explore the relationship between two sets of variables: input or *predictor* variables, and outcome or *dependent* variables. We wanted to know which variables best predict outcomes such as engagement and performance.

The predictor variables are seven of the items that assessed perceptions of managers and senior managers:

- senior managers' vision of where the organisation is going

- managers' respect for employees

- managerial commitment to the organisation

- opportunities for upward feedback

- feeling well-informed about what is going on in the organisation

- ability of managers to deal with issues fairly

- credibility of information.

The seven items were chosen because they represent distinct areas of leadership and organisational practice. Each item is itself representative of several issues. For example, a perception that managers are committed to the organisation could encompass a manager's productivity, how positively they speak about the organisation, and whether they are willing to go the extra mile to do their job well. The breadth of each item needs to be considered when looking at the results of the regression analyses.

These variables were examined in relation to engagement with work, which has three components:

Engagement with work

- cognitive engagement

- emotional engagement

- physical engagement

Next, analysis focused on the relationship between the six leadership and management variables, and the three facets of engagement (the input variables) and two dependent or outcome variables:

Performance

- appraisal rating

Intentions to leave

- intention to quit

Regression analysis examines the likelihood of association between variables, that is, the degree to which the relationship is likely to have occurred by chance. A significant relationship is one that is highly unlikely to have occurred by chance and is therefore important. Regression also shows the direction of association between variables. A positive association is when a high score on one variable is associated with a high score on the second variable, for example high levels of perceived meaningfulness of work being associated with high levels of engagement with work. A negative association is when a high score on one variable is associated with a low score on the other variable, for example high levels of perceived engagement with work being associated with a lack of intention to leave an organisation. To sum up, regression equations show which of the input variables best predict the value of the dependent variable.

ENDNOTES

1   MAY, D.R., GILSON, R.L. and HARTER, L.M. (2004). The psychological conditions of meaningfulness, safety and availability and the engagement of the human spirit at work. *Journal of Occupational and Organizational Psychology*. Vol 77. pp11–37.

2   WARR, P.B., COOK, J.D. and WALL, T.D. (1979). Scales for the measurement of some work attitudes and aspects of psychological well-being. *Journal of Occupational Psychology*. Vol 52. pp129–148.

3   WARR, P.B. (1987) *Work, employment and mental health*. Oxford: Oxford University Press.

    WARR, P. B. (1990). The measurement of well-being and other aspects of mental health. *Journal of Occupational Psychology*. Vol 63. pp193–210.